KATHERINE PARR

The Guided Tour Series

Anne Bradstreet: A Guided Tour of the Life and Thought of a Puritan Poet, by Heidi L. Nichols

J. Gresham Machen: A Guided Tour of His Life and Thought, by Stephen J. Nichols

Jonathan Edwards: A Guided Tour of His Life and Thought, by Stephen J. Nichols

Katherine Parr: A Guided Tour of the Life and Thought of a Reformation Queen, by Brandon G. Withrow

Martin Luther: A Guided Tour of His Life and Thought, by Stephen J. Nichols

Pages from Church History: A Guided Tour of Christian Classics, by Stephen J. Nichols

Stephen J. Nichols, series editor

KATHERINE PARR

A Guided Tour of the Life and Thought of a Reformation Queen

BRANDON G. WITHROW

P&R PUBLISHING

P.O. BOX 817 • PHILLIPSBURG • NEW JERSEY 08865-0817

Page design by Lakeside Design Plus

Printed in the United States of America

Library of Congress Cataloging-in-Publication Data

Withrow, Brandon.
  Katherine Parr : a guided tour of the life and thought of a Reformation queen / Brandon G. Withrow.
    p. cm. — (The guided tour of church history series)
  Includes bibliographical references and index.
  ISBN 978-1-59638-117-9 (pbk.)
  1. Catharine Parr, Queen, consort of Henry VIII, King of England, 1512–1548. 2. Catharine Parr, Queen, consort of Henry VIII, King of England, 1512-1548—Literary art. 3. Catharine Parr, Queen, consort of Henry VIII, King of England, 1512-1548--Religion. 4. Reformation—England—Sources. 5. Great Britain—History—Henry VIII, 1509–1547—Biography. 6. Queens—Great Britain—Biography. I. Catharine Parr, Queen, consort of Henry VIII, King of England, 1512-1548. Prayers or medytacions. II. Catharine Parr, Queen, consort of Henry VIII, King of England, 1512-1548. Lamentacion of a synner. III. Title.
  DA333.P3W58 2009
  942.05'2092—dc22
  [B]
                                        2008049657

To my mother, who taught me that women are human,
and to my wife, who continues the lesson

CONTENTS

ILLUSTRATIONS

FOREWORD

S
o few people wish to see Queen Katherine Parr, sixth wife of King Henry VIII, in her true colors. While it is accurate to say that she was an advocate of the "New Learning," which seems to cover Renaissance principles as much as Reformation principles, and while it is true that her end, dying in childbirth from her quite completely unreliable "true love" Thomas Seymour, could be interpreted as a triumph of the human love affair over the divine Spirit, this book confirms overwhelmingly that Katherine was to her core a woman of consuming religious ardor.

Such misconstruction has always sullied the landscape of English Reformation scholarship. Secular people do not wish to see in the Reformation the importance of the religious ideas that fueled it. Secular historians generally wish to paint it as a political revolution selecting religious ideas to cover over issues of *Machtpolitik*. Religious people have been more open to the voices of the participants themselves. This is to say, religious people recognize in characters such as Katherine Parr characters like themselves. For religious people, the theological issues of a thing always trump the sociological and political sides to it. For secular people, it is usually the other way around.

The histories of Katherine Parr have reflected the same duality. If a commentator is sympathetic to her authentic religious voice, that sympathy comes out in the treatment. If not, a text such as her *Lamentation* is regarded as formulaic or as part of a genre or as simply repeating commonplaces. Yet a quick reading of Katherine's text will dispel that notion absolutely. Her book, one of the few books written by women in the early modern period, defies any reduction to a type or category. *The Lamentation* is a distilled and almost overwhelming religious confession of a personal, if not classically evangelical, religious experience.

A few years ago, I tried to acquire a copy of this book. The only source where it appeared was a nineteenth-century edition of the British Reformers. So we had to send for it from far away. Brandon Withrow has now accomplished the inestimable service of making this important text available to us all again. The more texts of this kind that can be made accessible to the common reader, the more cost will be involved for those historians who aspire to de-theologize the English Reformation. Katherine's short book gives the lie to any construction of key participants in those consequential events of the mid-sixteenth century that fails to do justice to their evangelical convictions.

In short, Mr. Withrow's edition is much needed. It is needed not only for the scholarly community, and not only for the feminist community, for whom Katherine is a powerful if counterintuitive progenitor (which is to say, she used "feminine wiles" to influence King Henry). It is needed also for the common reader, and for the reader in search of religious role models who were also thoroughly human.

Read the book, say her prayers, discover Queen Katherine's story—and I believe you will know a most important truth about the Reformation in England.

Paul F. M. Zahl

ACKNOWLEDGMENTS

Bringing back into print a beloved but long-forgotten work such as Queen Parr's is a tedious (though rewarding) task, and therefore the assistance of others cannot be overestimated and must not be left unacknowledged. Foremost, I say thank you to my dedicated and forgiving wife, Mindy, who while working hard to put me through my Ph.D. program did not flinch at the prospect of discussing and proofing yet another manuscript that was not my dissertation. She is a constant source of strength for me, and without her these pages would be blank. My gratitude also belongs to Emily Sirinides of the Montgomery Library at Westminster Theological Seminary for her willingness to search far and wide for those hard-to-locate interlibrary loan sources. I have been edified by the forever gracious spirit of the Very Rev. Dr. Paul F. M. Zahl, former dean of Trinity Episcopal School for Ministry (Ambridge, Pennsylvania) and former dean of Cathedral Church of the Advent (Birmingham, Alabama), whose enthusiastic comments on the manuscript confirmed the value of its publication. Last, but far from least, I am grateful for the friendship of Dr. Stephen J. Nichols, who brought to life the Guided Tour series and became a favorite visitor of mine as I sat strapped to my study carrel in the Montgomery Library during the dissertation years. Like Parr's, his writing continues to bless the church.

INTRODUCTION: WHY READ KATHERINE PARR?

The life of Katherine Parr could have been simply a footnote to the Tudor rule. She was the daughter of a respectable, though not the most prominent, family in England. Had she not been widowed twice before becoming queen, she would probably have led a life of relative obscurity. Being the wife of Henry VIII, however, does not lend itself to simple and quiet living. Katherine rose to the highest position of power that a woman could have in England, and she used that power to bring about lasting change. She was also one of only a dozen English women in a hundred-year period to publish not just one, but two books and several prayers.

More than just a writer, she was a religious and cultural reformer who pressed a king for change, and nearly lost her life in trying. With so many of Henry's previous wives either discarded or executed, Katherine's proddings for reform were serious risks. Nevertheless, she championed the language of the people, encouraged academia to put Christ before Plato, urged Henry to bring England closer to the Reformation, commissioned scholarly translations of Erasmus, and brought a royal English family together. In Katherine's day, her books became examples of the bold Reformation spirit. Her brilliant mind captured the souls of her people and the respect of the Reformers themselves.

Despite her accomplishments and popularity in her day, this reformer continues to be passed over by modern readers. Until now, her published writings have been available to the modern audience only in the form of facsimile. For certain, the old English text, terribly long paragraphs, and archaic terminology do not always make for pleasure reading, but Katherine's trust in grace, colorful meditations, and strong conviction are ripe for the modern audience. Her dedication to the cross of Christ is a theme that transcends a culture gap of nearly five centuries, and her fervent spirituality and passion demonstrate that the Reformation was not limited to the ivory tower, but played itself out in real and practical ways.

As a historical figure, Katherine offers us more than just a look into the trials and struggles of the Protestant Reformation; she also gives us a picture of what it was like to be a woman of influence and conviction in such a dangerous age. She had to overcome not only the restricted life of a closet reformer (difficult no matter who you are), but also the cultural restrictions placed on her because of her gender. If fighting for the Protestant faith was not complicated enough, she had to overcome a husband who was not only the king, but also the newly proclaimed "supreme head of the church" in England. He was also not too fond of a wife who, to his perception, thought herself to be a "doctor."

Part One of this volume tells the Parr family's story, including Katherine's unexpected rise to power. It looks at her education and theological evolution, as well as at a plot hatched against her by enemies that nearly led to her death and to her placement in the annals of Henry's failed marriages. Ending with her tragic death as a result of the traumatic birth of her daughter, these pages are a glimpse into the drama of one who dared to put her people on a brighter path.

Part Two presents selected writings of Katherine, each with a brief introduction. These writings include Katherine's first book, *Prayers or Meditations*. With vibrant language, Katherine calls the reader to awaken, trust in Christ, forsake sin, and find forgiveness. A writer with mixed influences from Augustine to Erasmus to Luther, Katherine shows in this book that she is dedicated to an enduring and mystical relationship with Christ. Following this piece is Katherine's openly Protestant call for reform in England in the form of a spiritual autobiography known as *The Lamentation or Complaint of a Sinner*. Here Katherine calls Christians to forsake the "bishop of Rome." "For he is a persecutor of the gospel and grace," she writes; "he deceiveth and robbeth under Christ's mantle." Katherine urges Christians to learn from her personal failures, which she laments, and to find solace in the mercy and grace of the cross. Finally, this section closes with select letters from and to Katherine. These writings reveal her as a leader, a lover, and a mother.

This biographical introduction and the selected writings portray Katherine Parr, the person. She is not merely a historical figure; she is a thoughtful Christian whose works, as they did then and should now, raise one's senses to Christ and demand a response.

PART ONE

KATHERINE PARR'S LIFE

1

REFORMATION QUEEN: THE LIFE AND MIND OF KATHERINE PARR

The young girl, sitting in her father's study, with crossed legs and pen in hand, scribbling her name in the margins of his books, may not have caught the attention of most people. Noble girls were expected to learn the basics, but children were still children. It was said that as a girl Katherine had her palm read and was told that she would one day rise to great power. Whether or not the story is apocryphal no one knows for sure, but she certainly had hopes that one day she would be important. As she would write near the end of her life: "Christ came to serve his brethren, and I coveted to rule over them." Despite her hopes, the death of her father put her family in serious financial hardship. Her dowry was not impressive, and she would not have been voted "most likely to be queen."

For the Parr name to rise to the second-highest position in the land was no small accomplishment, even if Katherine could not have planned it. From their earliest years, the Parrs struggled to climb the ladder of power. The first Parr, Sir William (1350–1404), owned a meager portion of the villa of Parr. Having served as a knight for

FIG. 1.1 KATHERINE PARR AND HER TIMES

1478	Thomas Parr born
1508	Thomas Parr marries Maude Greene
1509	Henry VIII becomes king
1509	Henry VIII marries Catherine of Aragon
ca. 1512	Katherine Parr born
1512	Michelangelo completes Sistine Chapel
1516	Birth of Princess Mary
1517	Thomas Parr dies
1517	Martin Luther posts "95 Theses" in Wittenberg
1521	Martin Luther excommunicated by Pope Leo X
ca. 1525	Birth of Katherine Howard
1526	Katherine Parr marries Lord Borough
1526	William Tyndale publishes English New Testament
1527	Henry VIII seeks annulment of his marriage to Catherine of Aragon
1528	Lord Borough dies
1529	Maude (Greene) Parr dies
1533	Thomas Cranmer becomes Archbishop of Canterbury
1533	Henry VIII marries Anne Boleyn
1533	Princess Elizabeth born
1534	Katherine Parr marries John Neville, the third Lord Latimer
1534	Church of England separates from Rome
1536	Anne Boleyn executed on the false charges of witchcraft, incest, and adultery on May 19; Henry marries Jane Seymour 11 days later.

John of Gaunt (the Duke of Lancaster and the famous protector of John Wyclif), William met Elizabeth de Roos (d. ca. 1392), a wealthy heir of her grandfather. It was a transaction that brought William a quarter of the barony of Kendal and its castle.

Keeping the land, however, would prove to be difficult for the Parrs. William's son, John (1382–1408), inherited the land after his father's death and married Agnes Crophill. Unfortu-

1536	John Calvin publishes the first edition of the *Institutes of the Christian Religion*
1536–37	Pilgrimage of Grace; Lord Latimer taken hostage
1537	Prince Edward born to Henry VIII and Jane Seymour; Jane dies from complications a few days later
1540	Henry VIII marries Anne of Cleves in January, annuls marriage July 9
1540	Henry VIII marries Katherine Howard on July 28
1542	Katherine Howard executed for adultery
1543	Lord Latimer dies
1543	Thomas Seymour courts Katherine Parr
1543	Henry VIII and Katherine Parr marry on July 12
1544	Katherine Parr becomes regent as Henry VIII fights in France
1545	*Prayers or Meditations* published
1545	Council of Trent begins
1546	Katherine Parr suspected of being Protestant by Stephen Gardiner and Thomas Wriothesley
1547	Henry VIII dies in January; Edward VI becomes king
1547	Katherine Parr and Thomas Seymour marry in April
1547	*The Lamentation or Complaint of a Sinner* published
1548	Katherine Parr gives birth to Mary on August 30
1548	Katherine Parr dies on September 5
1549	Thomas Seymour executed for treason on March 20

nately, upon his death, their son, Thomas (1407/8–61), was not yet a year old, and the family inheritance was given to Sir Thomas Tunstall of Thurland, Lancashire. By the time Thomas was of age, he had to reconstruct the Parr family influence all over again. Through cunning political maneuvering, Parr managed to gain two-thirds of the barony of Kendal (and make a significant amount of income from it), only to lose it again. But this hardly held him back—with perseverance and other significant connections, Parr was still able to climb the power ladder again.

It was his sons, William (1434–83) and John Parr (d. 1475), who brought the family name lasting influence. Skilled with building alliances, William married Elizabeth Fitzhugh (1462–1505), whose powerful family owned a large amount of land, and he fostered a risky loyalty to Edward IV. It was a prodigious move, and when the Fitzhugh line ended, William's son Sir Thomas (1478–1517) inherited half the barony of Kendal.

Thomas, through his cousin Cuthbert Tunstall, kept the Parr family in the inner circle of Henry VIII and eventually became a knight. His influence was greatest in northern England, where his acquisition of land continued. In 1508, Thomas married Maude, the youngest daughter of Sir Thomas Greene, and had three children, William (1513–71), Anne, and Katherine (1512/14–48). Katherine was no more than five years old when Thomas died in November 1517, leaving Maude to care for the children by herself.[1]

The Life of Katherine

The Parrs were fortunate in that, even after Thomas's death, they remained within the inner circle of Henry. That Katherine's grandmother, Elizabeth, had strong connections to Henry's grandmother, Margaret Beaufort, also helped. But despite the important family connections, the Parr money was not nearly strong enough to offer a substantial dowry.

1. For a helpful and concise Parr family history, see Rosemary Horrox, "Parr Family," in *Oxford Dictionary of National Biography: From the Earliest Times to the Year 2000*, vol. 42, *Osborne-Pate*, ed. H. C. G. Matthew and Brian Harrison (New York: Oxford University Press, 2004), 838. For a traditional view of Parr family history, see Anthony Martienssen, *Queen Katherine Parr* (New York: McGraw-Hill, 1973). Katherine's birth date varies from biographer to biographer. Some have placed it at 1512 (see Alison Weir, *The Six Wives of Henry VIII* [New York: Grove Press, 1991], 486).

Much is uncertain about the early years of Katherine's life. In 1526 Maude successfully arranged a marriage between Katherine and Edward, Lord Borough. Borough's wife had died when he was around sixty-three years old, leaving him with a family. He quickly sought to remarry, and Katherine, an attractive young woman, was his choice. "Like many girls in her position," writes biographer Alison Weir, "Katherine found herself a stepmother to children older than herself." In 1528 Lord Borough died, and Katherine became a teenaged widow. The following year, on May 20, 1529, Katherine buried her mother, Maude, in the church of the Blackfriars, London.[2]

Things began to look up again when, in 1534, Katherine married John Neville, the third Lord Latimer, a distant relative. Latimer had been married twice before, with the last Lady Latimer dying around 1526/27. He was of strong medieval ancestry and had already loyally served Henry, having been knighted at twenty years of age. In 1536–37, Latimer became an important figure in the Pilgrimage of Grace, considered one of the worst uprisings against Henry's religious policy in the history of his reign. As supporters of the old faith, the rebels did not welcome concessions to the Reformers. Latimer, a Catholic, did not immediately side with the rebels, but they eventually pressured him to play a leading role in the rebellion. This move could have cost him his life when other rebel leaders were executed had he not been pardoned by Henry. Katherine's position as Lady Latimer brought her into the adult life of court attendance, entertaining, and household management, and is one of the many direct connections she had to the king.

2. The following discussion draws from these works: Agnes Strickland, *Lives of the Queens of England from the Norman Conquest with Anecdotes of Their Courts*, vol. 4 (Philadelphia: Lea and Blanchard, 1848), 15–16, 24; Alison Weir, *The Six Wives of Henry VIII*, 489–91, 493; Alison Weir, *The Children of Henry VIII* (New York: Ballantine Books, 1996), 41–80.

In March 1543, after leading thousands of men to battle against the Scots, Lord Latimer fell sick and died. By that time Henry had married Katherine Howard, had executed her for adultery, and had set his eyes on Katherine Parr. But before the king had formally expressed an interest in her, Sir Thomas Seymour, a handsome, wealthy, ambitious, and devious man, had already caught Katherine's attention. The Seymour family was politically powerful and Thomas well

1.2 Queen Katherine Parr, engraving by J. Cochran after the painting by Holbein.

known as a self-serving charmer who preyed on the women of the court. He cast his spell on Katherine and won her engagement, but they were not to marry, since the king (her fourth cousin) had had his eyes on her first. Determined to have whatever and whomever he wanted, Henry interfered with the engagement by sending Thomas to Brussels as ambassador to the Netherlands. Thomas got the message, and though Katherine's heart was his, no woman of this period who valued her position or life would resist the king, and she finally gave in. On July 12, 1543, Henry and Katherine married in a private ceremony.

With execution as an alternative to divorce, it was dangerous to be the wife of Henry. Katherine, however, had a few benefits that his other wives did not, the foremost being that his son Edward, by his third wife, Jane Seymour, had already been born. Once Henry had satisfied his lust for an heir, he was ready to turn his attention toward finding a mate. By the time of his marriage to Katherine, Henry had three children under his care: Mary, daughter of his first wife, Catherine of Aragon; Elizabeth, daughter of his second wife, Anne Boleyn; and Edward. Anne Boleyn had been executed in 1536 under the false charges of witchcraft, incest, and adultery. Jane Seymour had died after giving birth to Edward, and Henry's fourth marriage to Anne of Cleves, whom he found unattractive, had been annulled without consummation. His fifth wife, Katherine Howard, had been executed for infidelity. But in Katherine Parr, Henry found a woman whom he could respect in his limited way. Even more, she won the trust of Henry's children and became a mother to them.

The Education of a Queen

Early historians of Parr emphasized Katherine's family connections with royalty, life as a young girl in the court, and a high education in the "New Learning." The New Learning first arrived in the English court around 1485 through Henry's grandmother Margaret, who actively encouraged the education of women, especially those of noble heritage. A humanist education, promoted by intellectual giants such as Thomas More, Juan Luis Vives, and Erasmus, included a study of the classics in the original languages, requiring a good reading knowledge of Greek, Latin, French, and Italian.

Anthony Martienssen, a biographer of Katherine, describes Margaret Beaufort as "tolerant, shrewd," and "immensely rich," financing "a succession of thinkers and teachers," endowing colleges at Oxford and Cambridge, and bringing her "powerful influence to bear on the Court in the cause of reform." Believing that women should hold prominent positions in public life, Beaufort, according to Martienssen,

> was a convinced believer in the duty of women to moderate the excesses and guide the destiny of the new bustling society which her son had begun to create. At that stage of history, women had begun to achieve a high degree of independence. They ran their own businesses, were accepted as members by many of the Craft Guilds, held property in their own right, and could follow almost any calling they chose. . . . True, they usually had to be wives or widows before they could enjoy their freedom, but they then tended to retain their maiden names as proof of their separate identity in business or public life.[3]

Because of this connection, biographers have traditionally argued that Katherine's family was influenced by Beaufort's promotion of the New Learning. When Henry VIII ascended

3. Martienssen, *Queen Katherine Parr*, 3.

to his father's throne, his grandmother's duties passed on to Henry's wife, Catherine of Aragon, and in charge of Catherine's court school was Katherine's mother, Maude.

What is known by some extant letters is that Maude had a strong reputation as an educator, a skill demonstrated by her negotiation for Katherine's marriage to the son of Lord Scrope. Agreeing to speak on her behalf, a cousin of Thomas Parr (namely, Lord Dacre) wrote to Scrope. Maude offered an unimpressive dowry, to be repaid if the marriage was not carried out because of death, disagreement, or any other reason. Lord Dacre, realizing that Lord Scrope was not agreeable to these terms, placed other selling points on the table, suggesting that before the marriage, Scrope could recoup any financial loss by letting his son board with Maude, who would supply his food and drink as well as his education. "For I assure you," wrote Dacre, that "he might learn with her as well as in any place—that I know, as well nurture, as French, and other languages, which *me seems* were a commodious thing for him."[4] Despite Maude's respectable reputation as an educator, Lord Scrope drove too hard a bargain, and the deal fell through.

During her youth, according to Martienssen, Katherine (along with Princess Mary) was educated by Juan Luis Vives, the New Learning extraordinaire who caught the attention of Catherine of Aragon. His book, *On the Education of Christian Women*, was dedicated to the queen, and she believed that he was just the person to tutor the girls at court.[5] No historical evidence, however, has been found to back up this claim, and Parr's relationship to Vives and the New Learning is a sticking point among modern historians, who argue that such a background is the concoction of biased scholarship.

4. Strickland, *Lives of the Queens of England*, 13–14 (Letter to Lord Scrope, July 13, 1524; Letter of Lord Dacre to Lord Scrope, December 15), emphasis added.
5. Martienssen, *Queen Katherine Parr*, 21.

As biographer Susan E. James points out, "besides the fact that there is no evidence that Vives actually taught the princess personally—or ever left Spain for that matter—Kateryn was four years older than Mary and in 1523, when Catherine of Aragon was hiring tutors for her daughter, Kateryn, at 11, was already well into her education."[6]

Modern biographers have attempted to clean up perceived misconceptions produced by the idealistic portrait of the young queen. Over forty years ago, historian C. Fenno Hoffman Jr. challenged the traditional view of Katherine's classical education. Two decades later, Retha M. Warnicke also disputed certain received opinions on Katherine in her book *Women of the English Renaissance and Reformation*, arguing that "sympathetic biographers have exaggerated" her educational background.[7]

Hoffman agrees that Katherine had the benefit of an education but finds no evidence that she was classically trained with all the pomp of nobility, as is usually claimed. To prove this point, Hoffman points to a letter from Prince Edward to Katherine in June 1546, in which he compliments her on her progress in Latin. This is an indication, according to Hoffman, that Katherine probably did not know Latin well (knowledge of which is a hallmark of a classical education).[8] But as Hoffman notes, Katherine did have knowledge of French and Italian, two other important languages of the New Learning.

Another face could be put on this evidence, however, one that is more in keeping with Katherine's family heri-

6. Susan E. James, *Kateryn Parr: The Making of a Queen* (Aldershot, England: Ashgate, 1999), 28.

7. C. Fenno Hoffman Jr., "Catherine Parr as a Woman of Letters," *Huntington Library Quarterly* 23 (1960): 349–67; Retha M. Warnicke, *Women of the English Renaissance and Reformation* (Westport, CT: Greenwood Press, 1983), 94.

8. Hoffman, "Catherine Parr," 353; for this letter, see John Gough Nichols, *Literary Remains of King Edward the Sixth, Edited from His Autograph Manuscripts with Historical Notes and a Biographical Memoir*, vol. 1 (New York: Burt Franklin, 1857), 16–17 (Letter 17).

tage and later zeal for education. Hoffman assumes too much by concluding that Edward's comment on Katherine's progress in Latin testifies to her level of training. As James points out, "the queen's progress in Latin and in *belles-lettres* commended by Edward in the same letter may, in fact, refer not to lessons such as the young prince delighted in but to the translation project from Latin into English which the queen had at that moment in hand."[9] The work that Edward would be referring to was the translation of Erasmus's *Paraphrase of the Gospels* into English, a work that Katherine commissioned.

Another potential nail in the coffin of the traditional view is Katherine's letter to Cambridge in 1545, in which Katherine seems to acknowledge both her poor Latin and her disapproval of classical texts. Previously, Cambridge had requested—by a letter written in Latin—the queen's intervention before the king. Katherine's response, according to Warnicke, speaks to her understanding of Latin and her view of the classics:

> Your letters I have received, presented on all your behalfs by Mr Doctor Smith, your discreet and learned advocate. And as they be Latinly written, which is so signified unto me by those that be learned in the Latin tongue, so (I know) you could have uttered your desires and opinions familiarly in your vulgar tongue, aptest for my intelligence: albeit you seem to have conceived rather partially than truly a favourable estimation both of my going forward and dedication to learning. . . .
>
> . . . And for as much (as I do hear) all kind of learning doth flourish amongst you in this age, as it did amongst the Greeks at Athens long ago, I desire you all not so to hunger for the exquisite knowledge of profane learning, that it may be thought the Greeks' University was but transposed, or

9. James, *Kateryn Parr*, 32.

now in England again revived, forgetting our Christianity, since their excellency only did attain to moral and natural things. But rather I gently exhort you to study and apply those doctrines as means and apt degrees to the attaining and setting forth the better Christ's reverent and most sacred doctrine: that it may not be laid against you in evidence, at the tribunal of God, how you were ashamed of Christ's doctrine: for this Latin lesson I am taught to say of Saint Paul, *non me pudet evangelii.*[10]

Warnicke argues from this that Katherine "deplored the study of pagan literature," which, if true, strongly suggests that she had not been trained under the New Learning.[11]

Despite Katherine's strong rebuke in this letter, there is another possible interpretation. She could be understood as not rejecting the natural and moral philosophy of Plato as much as encouraging Cambridge professors to give Scripture its top priority—a trademark of Reformation thought. Because this letter is written during a time in which Katherine is slowly coming to accept Protestant theology, the emphasis on Scripture would make sense. It does not appear that the mere study of pagan literature bothered her; rather, it was its position over divinity, the queen of sciences. If Cambridge was to be known for anything, in her estimation, it should primarily be seen as a school of divinity.

10. Quoted in John Strype, *Ecclesiastical Memorials Relating Chiefly to Religion and the Reformation of It and the Emergencies of the Church of England under King Henry VIII, King Edward VI, and Queen Mary I with Large Appendixes, Containing Original Papers, Records, &c.*, vol. 2.2 (Oxford: Clarendon Press, 1822), 337–38.

11. Warnicke, *Women of the English Renaissance and Reformation*, 94. Contrary to this opinion, Katherine owned a heavily used copy of a volume by the Renaissance humanist Petrarch (Hoffman, "Catherine Parr," 353). See also John Gough Nichols, *Literary Remains of King Edward the Sixth, Edited from His Autograph Manuscripts with Historical Notes and a Biographical Memoir*, vol. 2 (New York: Burt Franklin, 1857), cccxxvi.

1.3 The Hierarchy of the Sciences as conceived by medieval thought, from the Berri Bible. From the bottom left, second row up, Avicenna, Socrates, and Plato. At the top of the hierarchy are God the Father and the crucified Christ.

As to her Latin, Katherine's inclusion of Paul's words in Latin ("I am not ashamed of the gospel") at the end of the letter is but a small sampling of her many references and translations of the Latin biblical text into English in her book *The Lamentation or Complaint of a Sinner* (1547/48). It is more likely that she was feigning humility, especially given the reputation of the scholars of Cambridge and their honoring her with a letter in Latin to begin with. It appears that they had no reason to believe her incapable of reading it.

Her education in Latin was strong enough that in 1544, when Henry campaigned in France, he turned regency over to her. Only one other wife of Henry had this privilege: the promoter of New Learning, Catherine of Aragon. To effectively carry out her role as regent and handle the country's business, Katherine would have to be capable of reading many languages. Henry could hardly have turned the empire over to a woman who could not read basic correspondence in Latin, a favorable form of letter writing in that day. She would have been at the mercy of the integrity of those around her to translate and respond in kind, not only accurately, but also without any agenda set against the king in his absence.

Even more to the point, the Parr family maintained many intellectual connections. For example, Thomas Parr was friends with Roger Ascham and Thomas More (an in-law to the Parr family and friend of Erasmus). With Cuthbert Tunstall as one of the greater influences over the widowed Maude Parr, and "given the scholarly proclivities of those who had the organization of the Parr children's education," argues James, "the standard adhered to would seem to have been high." In their schoolroom at home, when Katherine was a child, she and her siblings read their father's copy of *Horae ad Usum*

Sarum. A dedication to her uncle William appears in the volume in Katherine's childish handwriting, next to a woodcutting of her patron saint.[12] Latin seems to have been a part of their curriculum. A revised picture of her education may not necessarily include her education in the prestigious court itself (based on the evidence), but it does appear that the New Learning model found its way into Katherine's home.

A Reformer of Culture and Religion

The queen also took a keen interest in bringing the language of Christianity into the common tongue. While there appears to be evidence that Katherine used and encouraged the use of Latin, it seems that she preferred English, especially as a pedagogical tool. From early on, Katherine took an interest in the writings of Erasmus. She found them to be important enough that she received permission to procure a translation team with the sole purpose of translating Erasmus's *Paraphrase* into English for her people. She was also the patron of other translation projects, notably a treatise written by Margaret of Navarre.

That she wanted to communicate with the layperson and believed in providing for the laity's religious education in the people's tongue is even clearer by her own writings. The majority of her letters are in English. Besides one poem in French, her two published works, popularly known as *Prayers or Meditations* and *The Lamentation or Complaint of a Sinner*, are both in English. Moreover, when Henry waged war in France, he directed Thomas Cranmer to "revive the Catholic custom of holding processions through villages and towns to pray for 'the miserable state of Christendom,'" but allowed Cranmer to conduct these prayers in English. The idea of

12. James, *Kateryn Parr*, 26, 30.

prayers in English excited the queen so much that she contributed a prayer on behalf of the soldiers in France:

> Our cause being now just, and being enforced to enter into war and battle, we most humbly beseech Thee, O Lord God of Hosts, so to turn the hearts of our enemies to the desire of peace, that no Christian blood be spilt; or else grant, O Lord, that with small effusion of blood and to the little hurt

1.4 Thomas Cranmer (1489–1556), Archbishop of Canterbury, engraving by W. Holl after the painting by "Gerbicus Flicciis," or Gerlach Flicke (ca. 1545).

and damage of innocents, we may to Thy glory obtain victory. And that the wars being soon ended, we may all with one heart and mind, knit together in concord and unity, laud and praise Thee.[13]

She was, in this way, a cultural reformer, accomplishing what many such as William Tyndale had only dreamed.

But was Katherine a reformer of religion as well when she became queen? Early biographers and admirers often portray Katherine as an unabashedly Reformed queen when she entered the throne in 1543. This portrayal is largely derived from the high praise Katherine receives from John Foxe in his popular *Acts and Monuments*. It is true that Katherine left the throne as a Protestant calling for reformation, but initially she was, to be precise, more a follower of Erasmus.

Her life, before her marriage to Henry, does not leave much room for Reformation influence. She was very young during her short-lived marriage to Lord Borough, who, it seems, had some Reformation connections, but exactly how Reform-minded he was is uncertain.[14] While it is possible that during her time as a Latimer Katherine encountered Reformed ideas, there is no proof. It is usually argued that when Latimer moved to London, she was exposed to the Reformation, entertaining the likes of Miles Coverdale, Hugh Latimer, and John Parkhurst. There is no evidence that she had strong connections to these men at this time, either. There is also no reason to think that she changed her opinions about religion during her engagement to Thomas Seymour. He was not a religious person

13. Quoted in Martienssen, *Queen Katherine Parr*, 179–80.
14. Historians disagree about which Edward, Lord Borough, Katherine married. Some have thought it was the grandfather Borough, while others have believed it was the younger, grandson Edward. For more information, see James, *Kateryn Parr*, 60–62.

in any real sense of the word, and he honored only two sacraments: power and money.

Significant changes in Katherine's religious life began after she married Henry. At that time she came into contact with John Parkhurst, who had written Latin verses in honor of Katherine and Henry's visit to Oxford. He also came highly recommended from Katherine, the Duchess of Suffolk, who had hired Parkhurst as her chaplain some time before.[15] Queen Katherine took Parkhurst on as her chaplain, in which position he remained for the rest of her life. Parkhurst's sympathies with Reformed nonconformists probably helped serve as flint for her conversion to Protestantism.

Greater theological evolution occurred only a year later when Henry left Katherine as regent. As Diarmaid MacCulloch points out, while "the precise timing of her change of views is not clear," it is interesting that in 1544, while Henry was away, she may have been "in daily contact with Cranmer as she fulfilled her duties as Regent."[16] This suggestion is not without merit. When Henry commissioned the queen with regency, he ordered Cranmer to serve as one of her advisers.[17] Cranmer's inclusion in this list implies that there would be plenty of need for her to consult his opinions. It is probably here that she fostered a relationship with him, eventually leading to her intentional pressuring of Henry for greater reforms in the following year.

Around this time, Katherine drafted and published her *Prayers or Meditations*, a devotional work with influences

15. William P. Haugaard, "Katherine Parr: The Religious Convictions of a Renaissance Queen," *Renaissance Quarterly* 22 (1969): 350.

16. Diarmaid MacCulloch, *Thomas Cranmer: A Life* (New Haven: Yale, 1996), 327.

17. James Gairdner and R. H. Brodie, *Letters and Papers, Foreign and Domestic, of the Reign of Henry VIII, Preserved in the Public Record Office, the British Museum, and Elsewhere in England*, vol. 19.1 (London: Her Majesty's Stationery Office, 1903), 626.

ranging from Thomas à Kempis to Augustine to Erasmus. There is nothing specifically Protestant about this work, and in large part, it is Katherine's personalization of Thomas à Kempis, in that she, like many other writers in her day, borrows much of his language. (For more on Parr's use of Thomas's *The Imitation of Christ*, see the introduction to chapter 2 below.) In this work, Katherine's serious religious life was beginning to show through:

> Most benign Lord Jesus, grant me thy grace, that it may always work in me, and persevere with me unto the end.
>
> Grant me, that I may ever desire and will that which is most pleasant and most acceptable to thee.
>
> Thy will be my will, and my will be to follow always thy will.
>
> Let there be always in me one will and one desire with thee; and that I have no desire to will or not to will, but as thou wilt.
>
> Lord, thou knowest what thing is most profitable and most expedient for me.
>
> Give, therefore, what thou wilt, as much as thou wilt, and when thou wilt.[18]

Katherine was among only a handful of English women who had published anything within a century's time. "The Queen's book," writes Weir, "represented a real breakthrough in an age when only the most privileged women were fortunate enough to receive an education."[19]

This devotional work represents serious introspection. Her prayer "for my heart may not rest nor fully be pacified but only in thee" recalls Augustine's statement "our heart is

18. Katherine Parr, *Prayers or Meditations*, in Religious Tract Society, *Writings of Edward the Sixth, William Hugh, Queen Catherine Parr, Anne Askew, Lady Jane Grey, Hamilton, and Balnaves* (London: The Religious Tract Society, 1836), 15.

19. Weir, *The Six Wives of Henry VIII*, 514.

unquiet until it rests in you." A large percentage of these prayers emphasize her need for grace: "O Lord Jesus, make that possible by grace, which is impossible to me, by nature."[20] Such statements led Protestants after her to see

1.5 Henry VIII, from a portrait by Holbein (ca. 1542).

20. Parr, *Prayers or Meditations*, 18; Augustine of Hippo, *The Works of St. Augustine: A Translation for the 21st Century*, vol. 1.1, *The Confessions*, ed. John E. Rotelle, trans. Maria Boulding (Hyde Park, NY: New City Press, 1997), 39; Parr, *Prayers or Meditations*, 17.

this as a Protestant devotional, but as William P. Haugaard observes, "The contents of the book could not offend [the] Roman Catholic, Lutheran, or Calvinist. The prayers are not related to any liturgical observances but comprise a collection of purely private devotions."[21] Though this small Christian work is well worth reading for both Protestants and Catholics, it is neither explicitly Protestant nor Catholic. It does seem to appear at a time when Katherine was considering the former and moving away from the latter. After all, having published this in 1545, Katherine found herself distinctly tied to the Reformers a year later when Anne Askew was put on the rack.

Our primary record for this dramatic event is John Foxe's *Acts and Monuments*. While Foxe's records are far from "good history," and while Katherine does come across as a Queen Esther-like personality, there is a high probability that this record, in its general form, is closer to fact than some of his other historical accounts. Foxe, according to Haugaard, probably received the details of the incident from Parkhurst, a close friend.[22]

Anne Askew, a determined and outspoken Protestant, was charged with heresy by Bishop Stephen Gardiner and Lord Chancellor Thomas Wriothesley. The first time, she was arrested and released, but the second time she was not so fortunate. Gardiner, Wriothesley, and others engaged in a less-than-ethical search to squelch the Protestant advancement. Gardiner believed that Anne, one of many targets, had connections to important persons in the court. According to Anne's nephew, she was arrested when a letter she tried to send was intercepted. The letter implicated Katherine Parr as one whom she believed would be sympathetic to her cause. To add to the problem, while in prison, Anne

21. Haugaard, "Katherine Parr," 354.
22. Ibid., 352.

received money from members of the "queen's inner circle, as well as visits from the queen's own cousin, Nicholas Throckmorton."[23]

These connections brought Katherine under suspicion by Gardiner and Wriothesley, who sought to implicate the queen in the conspiracy.[24] In 1546 the queen and the king had such a close relationship that they discussed religion daily. From Foxe's record it appears that Katherine had strongly encouraged Henry to press for more of Cranmer's reforms and to end the "superstitions" of Rome. In her own way, Katherine was seeking to aid in the reformation of the church and was apparently successful at times. The king's openness to what Katherine had to say encouraged her to be bolder with each discussion. As Foxe recounts, she was

> oftentimes wishing, exhorting, and persuading the king, that as he had, to the glory of God, and his eternal fame, begun a good and a godly work in banishing that monstrous idol of Rome, so he would thoroughly perfect and finish the same, cleansing and purging his church of England clean from the dregs thereof, wherein as yet remained great superstition.[25]

But while the king enjoyed a good debate, his temper grew hotter as Katherine's discussions grew bolder and his counterpoints grew weaker. The king was adamant that a woman would not be his teacher. Gardiner and Wriothesley, keeping a close eye on Katherine because of her connections to Anne Askew, did not agree with the queen's encouragement

23. See James, *Kateryn Parr*, 269–74.

24. For a brief description of Anne Askew's interrogation, see Paul F. M. Zahl, *Five Women of the English Reformation* (Grand Rapids: Eerdmans, 2001), 27–40, 103–5.

25. John Foxe, *The Acts and Monuments of John Foxe: With a Life of the Martyrologist, and Vindication of the Work by the Reverend George Townsend*, vol. 5 (New York: AMS Press, 1965), 554.

of the king's reforms and looked hard for a way to keep her from bringing him closer to the Reformation. During this time the king suffered from an illness that affected his leg and his temperament, leaving him less than patient with Katherine's passionate discussions, and apparently open to suggestions.

One afternoon, the king's irritation outweighed his tolerance, and he broke off a serious conversation with Katherine on the Reformation. His anger with the queen took her and Gardiner by surprise. Gardiner, Foxe concludes, "thought, that if the iron were beaten whilst it was hot," he might be able to convince the king that the queen was a danger to his rule and should be removed from her position.[26] Gardiner had hoped to remove her from influence indefinitely. Whispering in the king's ear, he told Henry that Katherine thought she was wiser than he, that she sought to exalt herself to a doctor of theology, and that this had serious political, nearly treasonous ramifications, warranting death. Henry fumed with anger, and Gardiner, with Henry's permission, called for an investigation, sought to find banned books in the queen's library, and questioned the queen's ladies. The investigation began quietly, leaving Katherine completely in the dark. Eventually the king signed a bill of articles against the queen, and Gardiner set his plan into action.

Master Thomas Wendy, one of the queen's medical doctors, chose to disobey an order not to tell the queen. Foxe seems to imply that Henry told Wendy with the hopes that he would disobey orders and inform Katherine. Added to this, one of Henry's men dropped a crumpled copy of the articles against Katherine conveniently near her ladies-in-waiting. The implication was that Henry, in giving these orders against Katherine, was actually testing her

26. Ibid., 555.

loyalties—and keeping her life depended on passing that test. After being informed of the plot, the queen found herself bedridden in a deep depression. Hearing that Katherine was ill, Henry visited her bedside. She took the time to make her first appeal, confessing that she was afraid, "lest his majesty . . . had taken displeasure with her, and had utterly forsaken her." Despite the fire fueled by

1.6 Stephen Gardiner (ca. 1483–1555), Bishop of Winchester, engraving by P. A. Ganst.

Gardiner, the king, realizing her need, assured her with "sweet and comfortable words."[27]

Wendy came up with a plan by which Katherine could meet with the king and repair the situation between them before the action against her could take place. When the time came, she humbled herself before Henry:

> Your Majesty . . . doth right-well know, neither I myself am ignorant, what great imperfection and weakness by our first creation is allotted unto us women, to be ordained as inferior and subject unto man as our head; from which head all our direction ought to proceed: and that as God made man to his own shape and likeness, whereby he, being endued with more special gifts of perfection might rather be stirred to the contemplation of heavenly things, . . . so, also, made he woman of man, of whom and by whom she is to be governed, commanded, and directed; whose womanly weaknesses and natural imperfections ought to be tolerated, aided, and borne withal, so that, by his wisdom, such things as be lacking in her ought to be supplied.

Calling herself "a silly poor woman" and professing her inferiority, she apologized for seeking to be Henry's instructor and assured him that she sought only to have meaningful conversation to help him forget about his pain and to profit from his wisdom.[28] While her words were probably exaggerated to save her neck, they are not entirely out of step with her belief at the time that the husband was the spiritual head of the family. Nevertheless, it is important to note that despite her humility, the nature of Katherine's final book, *The Lamentation or Complaint of a Sinner*, demonstrates that she remained thoroughly convinced of her views.

27. Ibid., 558.
28. Quoted in ibid., 559.

Satisfied with her apology, the king comforted her: "Perfect friends we are now again, as ever at any time heretofore."[29] When Wriothesley showed up with guards at the scheduled time to take her away, he found only a king content to walk and talk with his wife as before. The plot was foiled, and he found himself the subject of the king's wrath in her stead, forbidden to ever enter his presence again. While Gardiner failed to implicate Katherine as a Protestant conspirator, her Protestantism would soon become public. Shortly after this incident, the queen finished her spiritual autobiography, *The Lamentation or*

1.7 Chancellor Thomas Wriothesley (1505–1550), first Earl of Southampton, engraved by H. Robinson.

29. Quoted in ibid., 560.

Complaint of a Sinner, which she strategically decided not to publish until after Henry died, in 1547. Gardiner's plot undoubtedly alerted the queen against publishing the work any sooner. In the *Lamentation*, Katherine bemoans her blindness (as well as that of others) to the truth of the gospel from the Reformation's perspective. Christ crucified for sin is a central theme. She begins the *Lamentation* with her repentance from her "evil and wretched former life."[30] The Protestant language shows up in her rejection of Catholic practices:

> I forsook the spiritual honouring of the true living God, and worshipped visible idols, and images made of men's hands, believing, by them, to have gotten heaven, yea to say the truth I made a great idol of myself, for I loved myself better than God. . . .
>
> . . . Furthermore, the blood of Christ was not reputed by me sufficient for to wash me from the filth of my sins; neither such ways, as he had appointed by his word. But I sought for such riffraff as the bishop of Rome hath planted in his tyranny and kingdom, trusting, with great confidence, by the virtue and holiness of them, to receive full remission of my sins.[31]

Throughout *The Lamentation* she continues to emphasize the value of Christ's death on the cross, arguing that it is only through knowing Christ as crucified that one can find peace with God. She clearly sees herself as one who formerly attempted to earn her eternal life—all the while trampling upon the work of Christ. In recounting true repentance, she recalls that she had neither "hope nor confidence

30. Katherine Parr, *The Lamentation or Complaint of a Sinner*, in Religious Tract Society, *Writings of Edward the Sixth, William Hugh, Queen Catherine Parr, Anne Askew, Lady Jane Grey, Hamilton, and Balnaves* (London: The Religious Tract Society, 1836), 32.
31. Ibid., 34.

in any creature, neither in heaven nor earth, but in Christ," her "whole and only Saviour."[32]

The Protestant emphasis on "faith only" and justification by faith, "not by deeds of the law," appears in the text: "Thus I feel myself to come, as it were, in a new garment before God; and now by his mercy to be taken as just and righteous, which of late without his mercy, was sinful and wicked; and by faith to obtain his mercy, the which the unfaithful cannot enjoy."[33] Henry is described as Moses, one who helped to lead his people out of the superstitious bondage of the Bishop of Rome, whom she likens to Pharaoh.

Interestingly, she confesses that she spent her life in darkness and that her conversion is recent: "I think no less, but many will wonder and marvel at this my saying, that I never knew Christ for my Saviour and Redeemer until this time."[34] With this in mind, it does not appear that Katherine strolled into the king's court a determined Protestant. Her marriage to him was short, but during that time she came under the influence of Protestants and did, in fact, embrace and promote Reformation teachings.

Katherine's Protestant Influence

As a Protestant queen, Katherine influenced both the king and his children, who would further the Protestant cause in England. Her influence over Henry is demonstrated by the recounting of her near-death experience at the hands of Gardiner. He was not simply looking to take out one queen; he was hoping to remove any and all who stood in the way of swaying the king and his children back

32. Ibid., 37.
33. Ibid., 39–40.
34. Ibid., 40.

toward Rome. In the view of her admirers, she stood on behalf of her people as Queen Esther had stood before Ahasuerus on behalf of the Jews.

How much influence did she have on the children? Historians disagree over the nature of her role in choosing tutors for Henry's children. The traditional view portrays Katherine as the Protestant queen who, given the task of choosing the tutor for Edward, made a political move, choosing Protestant tutors to rear the young prince. English historian J. K. McConica has pushed for such an interpretation,[35] and William Haugaard agrees: "Katherine Parr has usually missed her due in this matter, and McConica redresses the balance in his convincing argument that she was 'clearly the creative force' which brought together John Cheke, Ascham's student William Grindal, Anthony Cooke, and other reformminded scholars to share with Richard Cox the education of the young prince."[36] While Warnicke believes that Katherine had a strong relationship with and influenced Henry's children, she disagrees with Haugaard and McConica:

> Henry was clearly concerned with every detail of [Mary's] upbringing and was also responsible for the splendid education of his next two children, the Duke of Richmond [also known as Henry Fitzroy, the illegitimate son of Henry through an affair with Elizabeth Blount] and Princess Elizabeth. While the King sought advice from More and other scholars about tutors for his natural son, he provided the opportunity for his younger daughter, who was declared illegitimate in 1536 the year of Richmond's death, to learn Italian, French, Latin, and Greek

35. J. K. McConica, *English Humanists and Reformation Politics under Henry VIII and Edward VI* (Oxford: Clarendon Press, 1965), 216.
36. Haugaard, "Katherine Parr," 346–47.

from various instructors, among them William Grindal, a pupil of Roger Ascham.

Warnicke contends that the traditional belief that Queen Katherine appointed Edward's tutors is incorrectly based on the assumption that "she was both a committed Protestant and an experienced classical scholar at the time of her marriage to Henry."[37]

Although Katherine was not a committed Protestant when she married Henry, she was certainly under Protestant influence during her regency in 1544, and this was a

1.8 King Edward VI (1537–53), engraving by H. T. Ryall after the painting by Petworth (ca. 1547).

37. Warnicke, *Women of the English Renaissance and Reformation*, 93.

crucial year in the choice of tutors for Edward. During this time Henry was absorbed in preparation for war, and he did seek outside help in the responsibilities of choosing tutors for Edward. Katherine was no less an influence than other advisers, and the queen usually had the responsibility for the royal children's education. In his journal, Edward writes that he was "among the women" until the age of six years old (1543).[38] As Catherine of Aragon was responsible for Mary's education, Katherine Parr would have had responsibilities over Edward's upbringing.

In July 1544 Henry left for France, and Katherine, acting as regent, took care of all the remaining details of Edward's education. This does not mean, however, that Katherine handpicked all of Edward's tutors. Henry did leave particular instructions, as John Gough Nichols points out in his *Literary Remains of King Edward the Sixth*. State papers record that at this time "important alterations were made in the Prince's household" by the queen in the name of Henry, and many of these were instructions to the tutors. But whether this was Katherine's decision, using Henry's name as a formality, or truly Henry's direct orders to her is unknown. Nichols notes that "the Queen appears to have undertaken on this occasion the charge of all the royal family, as on the 25th of July she wrote from Hampton court to the King, 'My lord Prince and the rest of your Majesties children are all (thanks be to God) in very good health.'"[39]

Katherine's overall influence on the family was positive. Until her arrival, the family had been divided. Edward had no true concept of family, since Katherine Howard and Anne of Cleves had showed no interest. As Weir points out, when Katherine married Henry in 1543, Edward

38. Nichols, *Literary Remains*, 1:xl.
39. Ibid., 1:xxxix.

"quickly grew to love his stepmother, and in no time at all was referring to her as 'Mother,'" as is clear in his letters. Elizabeth also saw Katherine as her mother. When Elizabeth and her father had a falling-out in 1544, it was Katherine who helped to heal the rift between the two and convinced Henry to allow Elizabeth back to the court. When Grindal, Elizabeth's tutor, died, and Elizabeth wanted to have John Cheke as his replacement, she sought Katherine's permission before securing Cheke.[40] Both Edward and Elizabeth continually wrote letters to Katherine and sought her input. Katherine provided educational opportunities for all the children and even commissioned Mary and Elizabeth for some of her translation projects.

After Henry's death in 1547, Katherine and Admiral Thomas Seymour returned to their previous romantic relationship, eventually marrying. With her mother-hen approach to the children, Katherine tried to give Elizabeth a steady home life by bringing her to live with her and Thomas at Chelsea. During that time Katherine provided home worship services and prayer times that involved Elizabeth. Thomas, however, was known to be absent from any family worship, leaving it entirely in Katherine's hands. Hugh Latimer, Bishop of Worcester, in a sermon on Romans 15 preached before King Edward, commented on Seymour's absence: "I have heard say, when that good queen that is gone had ordained in her house daily prayer both before noon, and after noon, the admiral gets him out of the way, like a mole digging in the earth. He shall be Lot's wife to me as long as I live."[41]

40. Weir, *The Children of Henry VIII*, 14, 51.

41. Hugh Latimer, *The Works of Hugh Latimer, Sometime Bishop of Worcester, Martyr, 1555*, ed. George Elwes Corrie (Cambridge: Parker Society and University Press, 1844), 228.

One instance is particularly telling. Katherine was unaware that Thomas had had designs on Elizabeth before they were married. Elizabeth's time at the Seymour household was filled with Thomas's semi-covert attempts to bed her. As time passed and Thomas had seemingly won Elizabeth's heart, he became bolder and Katherine became suspicious. After finding him in many compromising situations with Elizabeth, and after having naively accepted his charming excuses, Katherine finally decided in 1548 that it was in Elizabeth's best interests (and her own) to remove her from the household and away from Thomas's influence. After Elizabeth left the household, she experienced a difficult illness, leaving many to speculate that she miscarried a child of Seymour. Elizabeth's guilt over her betrayal of Katherine prompted her to write letters, hoping to repair the relationship. Katherine continued to show nothing but concern for her, and her positive influence over Elizabeth remained.

Katherine seemed to have the best interests of Henry's children in mind. She instructed them, guided them, and hoped to provide a family for them. At Okinge, for example, where the children were under her care, a pestilence broke out, causing Katherine to seek their protection by decree:

> To make proclamation that, since, on the account of the plague, great danger might arise to her, the prince, and the king's other children, no person in whose house the plague has been, or who may have been with any infected person, or may have lived near any place where the infection had been, should go to court, or suffer any attendants on the court to enter his house where the infection is, under the queen's indignation and further punishment at her pleasure.

From Okinge[42]

42. Strickland, *Lives of the Queens of England*, 40.

While it may be uncertain as to her exact role in choosing their tutors, it is certain that she influenced their lives and education. It is no coincidence that Katherine's relationship with Edward and Elizabeth was stronger than her relationship to Mary, and it is both Edward and Elizabeth who take the Protestant Reformation to the next level during their reigns.

Katherine's Death

On August 30, 1548, at Sudeley Castle and now married to Thomas Seymour, Katherine gave birth to her only child, a daughter named Mary—but the celebration was cut short. Katherine suffered through a difficult labor and developed a high fever, dying six days later. Thomas Seymour returned

1.9 Thomas, Lord Seymour of Sudeley (ca. 1508–49), engraving by Thomas Wright after the painting by Holbein.

to the military, and underhandedly worked to unseat his brother, Edward Seymour, the Duke of Somerset and guardian to King Edward. On March 20, 1549, he lost his head under charges of treason. His infant daughter Mary was now without both parents and fell into a difficult life. At one point an act of Parliament removed her inheritance when she was eight months old. This was followed by another act sometime later reinstating her inheritance. Most historians believe that Mary died at a young age.

Katherine's journey to royalty was not easy, but armed with her education and empowered by her reforming views, as well as her Protestant convictions, she was able to move a king to make reforms, protect those in the Reformation cause, encourage the use of the vernacular in worship, contribute to the body of Protestant theology, and reinforce Protestant ideas in Henry's children, especially Edward— and all only within the few years between her conversion and death. As was once said of another queen, who knows whether she had not attained royalty "for such a time as this" (Est. 4:14)?

PART TWO

SELECTED WRITINGS OF KATHERINE PARR

THE AWAKENED QUEEN: *PRAYERS OR MEDITATIONS* (1545, 1547)

Prayers or Meditations represents a genre that is rare today. It is a poetic and mystical call for prayer and meditation. Written in the first person, the text presents Katherine as an example of one surrendering to Christ. It is full of passionate introspection, grieving, and rejoicing, with the cries of a searching soul bursting into print. In these pages, she asks Christ to "make that possible by grace, that is . . . impossible by nature." Katherine sees the Christian life as something that did not ultimately reside in the university library or in the pulpit, but in the heart that is directed toward God. This conviction is strongly expressed here, and because it was probably written just before Katherine's conversion to the Reformed faith, it reflects a change in her focus on the grace of God. One sees a woman who is achieving a spiritual awareness in her life that had never before existed.

C. Fenno Hoffman and Retha M. Warnicke note Katherine's borrowing of text from Thomas à Kempis's *The Imitation*

PRAYERS OR

Medytacions, wherein the
mynd is stirred, paciently to
suffre all afflictions here, to
set at nought the vayne pro-
speritee of this worlde, and
alwaie to longe for the euer-
lastynge felicitee: Collected
out of holy woorkes by
the most vertuous
and graciouse
Princesse
Kathe-
rine
quene of Englande,
Fraunce, and
Irelande.
Anno dñi
1547.

2.1 Title page of *Prayers or Meditations* (1547).

of Christ.[1] The scholarship of the day did not include modern standards of plagiarism, but Parr is doing something far different from simple plagiarism. As Janel Mueller points out, "Parr's subtle yet thorough redaction excises the monastic framework of the original work and makes its Christic affectivity equally accessible to pious laity of both genders." She was providing a "vernacular manual for private devotion to circulate along with the English translation of the Litany, a mainstay of public devotion." Though not specifically a Protestant at this time, in this way Katherine is picking up on the individual spirit of the Reformation age.[2]

This version of *Prayers or Meditations* is intended to accurately represent the original(s) and is primarily taken from the 1545 and 1547 editions. A few scattered words that are not found in today's dictionaries are defined in the footnotes. In addition, some spellings, punctuation, paragraphing, and capitalization have been updated. Following the text reprinted here are several prayers as they appeared in the 1547 version (an expansion of the first edition in 1545). Because of the book's popularity among the Reformed in England, approximately seventeen editions had appeared by 1640.[3]

PRAYERS OR MEDITATIONS

Wherein the mind is stirred, patiently to suffer all afflictions here, to set at nought the vain prosperity of this world, and always to long for the everlasting felicity: Collected out of holy

---

1. C. Fenno Hoffman Jr., "Catherine Parr as a Woman of Letters," *Huntington Library Quarterly* 23 (1960): 354; Retha M. Warnicke, *Women of the English Renaissance and Reformation* (Westport, CT: Greenwood Press, 1983), 93.

2. Janel Mueller, "Introductory Note," in *The Early Modern Englishwoman: A Facsimile Library of Essential Works, Part 1: Printed Writings, 1500–1640*, vol. 3, *Katherine Parr* (Aldershot, England: Scolar Press, 1996), xi; see also Janel Mueller, "Devotion as Difference: Intertextuality in Queen Katherine Parr's Prayers or Meditations (1545)," *Huntington Library Quarterly* 53 (1990): 171–97.

3. Mueller, "Introductory Note," xi.

works by the most virtuous and gracious princess Katherine,
Queen of England, France, and Ireland.

A.D. 1547.

"If ye be risen again with Christ, seek the things which are
above, where Christ sitteth on the right hand of God. Set
your affection on things that are above: and not on things
which are on the earth." [Col. 3:1–2]

Most benign Lord Jesus, grant me thy grace, that it may
always work in me, and persevere with me unto the end.

Grant me, that I may ever desire and will that which is
most pleasant and most acceptable to thee.

Thy will be my will, and my will be to follow always thy
will.

Let there be always in me one will and one desire with
thee; and that I have no desire to will or not to will, but as
thou wilt.

Lord, thou knowest what thing is most profitable and
most expedient for me.

Give, therefore, what thou wilt, as much as thou wilt, and
when thou wilt.

Do with me what thou wilt, as it shall please thee, and
shall be most to thine honour.

Put me where thou wilt, and freely do with me all things
after thy will.

Thy creature I am, and in thy hands, lead and turn me
where thou wilt.

Lo, I am thy servant, ready to do all things that thou
commandest: for I desire not to live to myself, but to thee.

Lord Jesus, I pray thee, grant me grace, that I never set my
heart on the things of this world, but that all worldly and
carnal affections may utterly die and be mortified in me.

Grant me above all things that I may rest in thee, and fully quiet and pacify my heart in thee.

For thou Lord, art the very true peace of heart, and the perfect rest of the soul, and without thee, all things art grievous and unquiet.

My Lord Jesus, I beseech thee, be with me in every place, and at all times, and let it be to me a special solace, gladly, for thy love, to lack all worldly solace.

And if thou withdraw thy comfort from me at any time, keep me, O Lord, from desperation, and make me patiently to abide thy will and ordinance.

O Lord Jesus, thy judgments art righteous, and thy providence is much better for me than all that I can imagine or devise.

Wherefore, do with me in all things as it shall please thee, for it may not be but well, all that thou doest.

If thou wilt that I be in light, be thou blessed: if thou wilt that I be in darkness, be thou also blessed.

If thou vouchsafe to comfort me, be thou highly blessed: if thou wilt I live in trouble and without comfort, be thou likewise ever blessed.

Lord, give me grace gladly to suffer whatsoever thou wilt shall fall upon me, and patiently to take at thy hand good and bad, bitter and sweet, joy and sorrow, and for all things that shall befall unto me, heartily to thank thee.

Keep me, Lord, from sin, and I shall then neither dread death nor hell.

O what thanks ought I to give unto thee, who hast suffered the grievous death of the cross, to deliver me from my sins, and to obtain everlasting life for me?

Thou gavest us most perfect example of patience, fulfilling and obeying the will of thy Father, even unto the death.

Make me, wretched sinner, obediently to use myself after thy will in all things, and patiently to bear the burden of this corruptible life.

For though this life be tedious, and as a heavy burden to my soul, yet nevertheless, through thy grace, and by example of thee, it is now made much more easy and comfortable than it was before thy incarnation and passion.

Thy holy life is our way to thee, and by following of thee we walk to thee who art our head and Saviour. And yet except thou hadst gone before, and showed us the way to everlasting life, who would endeavour himself to follow thee? Seeing we be yet so slow and dull, having the light of thy blessed example and holy doctrine to lead and direct us.

O Lord Jesus, make that possible by grace, that is to me impossible by nature.

Thou knowest well that I may little suffer, and that I am anon cast down and overthrown with a little adversity: wherefore, I beseech thee, O Lord, to strengthen me with thy Spirit, that I may willingly suffer for thy sake all manner of trouble and affliction.

Lord, I will acknowledge unto thee all mine unrighteousness, and I will confess to thee all the unstableness of my heart.

Oftentimes a very little thing troubleth me sore, and maketh me dull and slow to serve thee.

And sometimes I purpose to stand strongly, but when a little trouble cometh, it is to me great anguish and grief, and of a right little thing riseth a grievous temptation to me.

Yea, when I think myself to be sure and strong, and that (as it seemeth) I have the upper hand: suddenly I feel myself ready to fall with a little blast of temptation.

Behold, therefore, good Lord, my weakness, and consider my frailness, best known to thee.

Have mercy on me, and deliver me from all iniquity and sin, that I be not entangled therewith.

Oftentimes it grieveth me sore, and in manner confoundeth me, that I am so unstable, so weak, and so frail in resisting sinful motions.

Which, although they draw me not always to consent, yet nevertheless their assaults art very grievous unto me.

And it is tedious to me to live in such battle, albeit I perceive that such battle is not unprofitable unto me. For thereby I know the better myself, and mine own infirmities, and that I must seek help only at thy hands.

O Lord God of Israel, the lover of all faithful souls, vouchsafe to behold the labour and sorrow of me, thy poor creature.

Assist me in all things with thy grace, and so strengthen me with heavenly strength, that neither my cruel enemy, the fiend, neither my wretched flesh (which is not yet subject to the spirit), have victory or dominion over me.

O what a life may this be called where no trouble nor misery lacketh? where every place is full of snares of mortal enemies?

For one trouble or temptation overpassed, another cometh by and by, and the first conflict enduring, a new battle suddenly ariseth.

Wherefore, Lord Jesus, I pray thee, give me the grace to rest in thee above all things, and to quiet me in thee above all creatures, above all glory and honour, above all dignity and power, above all cunning and policy, above all health and beauty, above all riches and treasure, above all joy and pleasure, above all fame and praise, above all mirth and consolation, that man's heart may take or feel besides thee.

For thou, Lord God, art best, most wise, most high, most mighty, most sufficient, and most full of all goodness, most sweet, and most comfortable, most fair, most loving, most noble, most glorious, in whom all goodness most perfectly is.

And therefore, whatsoever I have besides thee, it is nothing to me: for my heart may not rest nor fully be pacified but only in thee.

O Lord Jesus, most loving spouse, who shall give me wings of perfect love, that I may fly up from these worldly miseries, and rest in thee?

O when shall I ascend to thee, and see and feel how sweet thou art?

When shall I wholly gather myself in thee, so perfectly that I shall not, for thy love, feel myself, but thee only, above myself, and above all worldly things, that thou mayest vouchsafe to visit me in such wise as thou dost visit thy most faithful lovers.

Now, I often mourn and complain of the miseries of this life, and with sorrow and great heaviness suffer them.

For many things happen daily to me which oftentimes trouble me, make me heavy, and darken mine understanding.

They hinder me greatly, and put my mind from thee, and so encumber me many ways, that I cannot freely and clearly desire thee, nor have thy sweet consolations, which with thy blessed saints art always present.

I beseech thee, Lord Jesus, that the sighings and inward desires of my heart may move and incline thee to hear me.

O Jesus, King of everlasting glory, the joy and comfort of all Christian people that art wandering as pilgrims in the wilderness of this world, my heart crieth to thee by still desires, and my silence speaketh unto thee, and saith: How long tarrieth my Lord God to come to me?

Come, O Lord, and visit me, for without thee I have no true joy; without thee my soul is heavy and sad.

I am in prison, and bound with fetters of sorrow, till thou, O Lord, with thy gracious presence, vouchsafe to visit me, and to bring me again to liberty and joy of spirit, and to show thy favourable countenance unto me.

Open my heart, Lord, that I may behold thy laws, and teach me to walk in thy commandments.

Make me to know and follow thy will, and to have always in my remembrance thy manifold benefits, that I may yield due thanks to thee for them.

But I acknowledge and confess for truth, that I am not able to give thee condign thanks for the least benefit that thou hast given me.

O Lord, all gifts and virtues that any man hath in body or soul, natural or supernatural, are thy gifts and come of thee, and not of ourselves, and they declare the great riches of thy mercy and goodness unto us.

And though some have more gifts than others, yet they all proceed from thee, and without thee the least cannot be had.

O Lord, I account it for a great benefit, not to have many worldly gifts, whereby the laud and praise of men might blind my soul, and deceive me.

Lord, I know that no man ought to be abashed or miscontent that he is in a low estate in this world, and lacketh the pleasures of this life, but rather to be glad and rejoice thereat.

For so much as thou hast chosen the poor and meek persons, and such as art despised in the world, to be thy servants and familiar friends.

Witness thy blessed apostles, whom thou madest chief pastors and spiritual governors of thy flock, who departed from the council of the Jews, rejoicing that they were counted worthy to suffer rebuke for thy name.

Even so, O Lord, grant that I thy servant may be as well content to be taken as the least, as others are to be greatest, and that I be as well pleased to be in the lowest place as in the highest, and as glad to be of no reputation in the world, for thy sake, as others are to be noble and famous.

Lord, it is the work of a perfect man never to sequester his mind from thee, and among many worldly cares to go without care: not after the manner of an idle or a dissolute person, but by the prerogative of a free mind, always minding heavenly things, and not cleaving by inordinate affection to any creature.

I beseech thee, therefore, my Lord Jesus, keep me from the superfluous cares of this world, that I be not disquieted with bodily necessities, and that I be not taken with the voluptuous pleasures of the world, or of the flesh.

Preserve me from all things which hinder my soul's health, that I be not overthrown with them.

O Lord God, who art sweetness unspeakable, turn into bitterness to me all worldly and fleshly delights, which might draw me from the love of eternal things, to the love of short and vile pleasures.

Let not flesh and blood overcome me, nor yet the world with his vainglory deceive me, nor the fiend with his manifold crafts supplant me: but give me spiritual strength in resisting them, patience in suffering them, and constancy in persevering to the end.

Give me, for all worldly delectations, the most sweet consolation of thy Holy Spirit, and for all fleshly love, endue my soul with fervent love of thee.

Make me strong inwardly in my soul, and cast out thereof all unprofitable cares of this world, that I be not led by unstable desires of earthly things, but that I may repute all things in this world (as they be) transitory, and soon vanishing away, and myself also with them drawing toward mine end.

For nothing under the sun may long abide, but all is vanity and affliction of spirit.

Give me, Lord, therefore, heavenly wisdom, that I may learn to seek and find thee, and above all things to love thee.

Give me grace to withdraw me from them that flatter me, and patiently to suffer them that unjustly grieve me.

Lord, when temptation or tribulation cometh, vouchsafe to succour me, that all may turn to my spiritual comfort, and patiently to suffer, and always to say, "Thy name be blessed."

Lord, trouble is now at hand, I am not well, but I am greatly vexed with this present affliction. O most glorious Father, what shall I do? Anguish and trouble are on every side; help now, I beseech thee, in this hour: thou shalt be lauded and praised when I am perfectly made meek before thee, and when I am clearly delivered by thee.

May it therefore please thee, to deliver me: for what may a most sinful wretch do? Or whither may I go for succour, but to thee?

Give me patience now at this time in all my troubles; help me, Lord God, and I shall not fear nor dread, what troubles soever fall upon me.

And now, what shall I say, but that thy will be done in me; I have deserved to be troubled and grieved: and therefore it behoveth, that I suffer as long as it pleaseth thee.

But would to God, that I might suffer gladly, till the furious tempests were overpassed, and that quietness of heart might come again.

Thy mighty hand, Lord, is strong enough to take this trouble from me, and to assuage the cruel assaults thereof, that I be not overcome with them, as thou hast oftentimes done before this time, that when I am clearly delivered by thee, I may with gladness say, "The right hand of him that is highest hath made this change."

Lord, grant me thy singular grace, that I may come thither where no creature shall hinder me, nor keep me from the perfect beholding of thee.

For as long as any transitory thing keepeth me back, or hath rule in me, I may not truly ascend to thee.

O Lord, without thee nothing may long delight or please. For if any thing should be liking and savoury, it must be through help of thy grace, seasoned with the spice of thy wisdom.

O everlasting Light, far passing all things, send down the beams of thy brightness from above, and purify and lighten the inward parts of my heart.

Quicken my soul and all the powers thereof, that it may cleave fast, and be joined to thee, in joyful gladness of spiritual ravishings.

O when shall that blessed hour come, that thou shalt visit me and gladden me with thy blessed presence, when thou shalt be to me all in all? Verily, until that time come, there can be no perfect joy in me.

But alas, mine old man, that is my carnal affections, live still in me, and are not crucified nor perfectly dead.

For yet striveth the flesh against the spirit, and moveth great battle inwardly against me, and suffereth not thy kingdom of my soul to live in peace.

But thou, good Lord, that hast the lordship over all, and power of the sea, to assuage the rages and surges of the same, arise and help me, destroy the power of mine enemies, which always make battle against me. Show forth the greatness of thy goodness, and let the power of thy right hand be glorified in me. For there is to me none other hope nor refuge, but in thee only, my Lord, my God; to thee be honour and glory everlasting.

O Lord, grant me that I may wholly resign myself to thee, and in all things to forsake myself, and patiently to bear my cross and to follow thee.

O Lord, what is man, that thou vouchsafest to have mind of him? and to visit him?

Thou art always one, always good, always righteous; and holily, justly, and blessedly disposing all things after thy wisdom.

But I am a wretch, and of myself always ready and prone to evil, and do never abide in one state, but many times do vary and change.

Nevertheless, it shall be better with me, when it shall please thee, for thou, O Lord, only art he that mayest help me, and thou mayest so confirm and establish me, that my heart shall not be changed from thee, but be surely fixed, and finally rest and be quieted in thee.

I am nothing else of myself but vanity before thee, an unconstant creature and a feeble: and therefore, whereof may I rightfully glory, or why should I look to be magnified?

Whoso pleaseth himself without thee, displeaseth thee: and he that delighteth in man's praisings, loseth the true praise before thee.

The true praise is to be praised of thee: and the true joy is to rejoice in thee.

Wherefore, thy name, O Lord, be praised, and not mine.

Thy works be magnified, and not mine, and thy goodness be always lauded and blessed.

Thou art my glory and the love of my heart; in thee shall I glory and rejoice, and not in myself, nor in any worldly honour or dignity, which to thy eternal glory compared is but a shadow and very vanity.

O Lord, we live here in great darkness, and are soon deceived with the vanities of this world, and are soon grieved with a little trouble: yet if I could behold myself well, I should plainly see that what trouble soever I have suffered, it hath justly come upon me, because I have often sinned, and griev-ously offended thee.

To me, therefore, confusion and despite is due: but to thee laud, honour, and glory.

Lord, send me help in my troubles, for man's help is little worth.

How often have I been disappointed, where I thought I should have found friendship? And how often have I found it where I least thought?

Wherefore it is a vain thing to trust in man, for the true trust and health of man is only in thee.

Blessed be thou, Lord, therefore, in all things that happen unto us, for we are weak and unstable, soon deceived, and soon changed from one thing to another.

O Lord God, most righteous judge, strong and patient, who knowest the frailty and malice of man, be thou my whole strength and comfort in all necessities, for mine own conscience, Lord, sufficeth not.

Wherefore, to thy mercy I do appeal, seeing no man may be justified, nor appear righteous in thy sight, if thou examine him after thy justice.

O blessed mansion of thy heavenly city: O most clear day of eternity, which the night may never darken.

This is the day, always clear and merry, always sure, and never changing its state.

Would to God this day might shortly appear and shine upon us, and that these worldly fantasies were at an end.

This day shineth clearly to thy saints in heaven, with everlasting brightness, but to us pilgrims on earth it shineth obscurely, and as through a mirror or glass.

The heavenly citizens know how joyous this day is: but we outlaws, the children of Eve, weep and wail the bitter tediousness of our day, that is, of this present life, short and evil, full of sorrow and anguish, where man is oftentimes defiled with sin, encumbered with affliction, disquieted with troubles, wrapped in cares, busied with vanities, blinded with errors, overcharged with labours, vexed with temptations, overcome with vain delights and pleasures of the world, and grievously tormented with penury and need.[4]

O, when shall the end come of all these miseries?

When shall I be clearly delivered from the bondage of sin?

When shall I, Lord, have only mind on thee, and fully be glad and merry in thee?

When shall I be free without hindrance, and be in perfect liberty, without grief of body and soul?

When shall I have peace without trouble? peace within and without, and on every side steadfast and sure?

O Lord Jesus, when shall I stand and behold thee? and have full sight and contemplation of thy glory?

When shalt thou be to me all in all? And when shall I be with thee in thy kingdom, that thou hast ordained for thine elect people from the beginning?

I am left here poor, and as an outlaw, in the land of mine enemies, where daily are battles and great misfortunes.

Comfort mine exile, assuage my sorrow, for all my desire is to be with thee.

It is to me an unpleasant burden, what pleasure soever the world offereth me here.

I desire to have inward fruition in thee, but I cannot attain thereto.

I covet to cleave fast to heavenly things, but worldly affections pluck my mind downward.

I would subdue all evil affections, but they daily rebel and rise against me, and will not be subject unto my spirit.

Thus I, wretched creature, fight in myself, and am grievous to myself, while my spirit desireth to be upward, and contrary, my flesh draweth me downward.

4. This passage is a good example of Katherine's borrowing. Compare with chapter 48 of *Imitation*.

O what suffer I inwardly: I go about to mind heavenly things, and straight a great rabble of worldly thoughts rush into my soul.

Therefore, Lord, be not long away, nor depart in thy wrath from me.

Send me the light of thy grace, destroy in me all carnal desires.

Send forth the hot flames of thy love to burn and consume the cloudy fantasies of my mind.

Gather, O Lord, my wits and the powers of my soul together in thee, and make me to despise all worldly things, and by thy grace strongly to resist and overcome all motions and occasions of sin.

Help me, thou everlasting truth, that no worldly guile nor vanity hereafter have power to deceive me.

Come also, thou heavenly sweetness, and let all bitterness of sin flee far from me.

Pardon me, and forgive me, as oft as in my prayer my mind is not surely fixed on thee.

For many times I am not there where I stand or sit, but rather there whither my thoughts carry me.

For there I am, where my thought is, and there as customably is my thought, there is that that I love.

And that oftentimes cometh into my mind that by custom pleaseth me best, and that delighteth me most to think upon.

Accordingly as thou dost say in thy gospel, "Where a man's treasure is, there is his heart" [Matt. 6:21].

Wherefore, if I love heaven I speak gladly thereof, and of such things as be of God, and of that that appertaineth to his honour, and to the glorifying of his holy name.

And if I love the world, I love to talk of worldly things, and I joy anon in worldly felicity, and sorrow and lament soon for worldly adversity.

If I love the flesh, I imagine oftentimes that that pleaseth the flesh.

If I love my soul, I delight much to speak and to hear of things that are for my soul's health.

And whatsoever I love, of that I gladly hear and speak, and bear the images of them still in my mind.

Blessed is that man, who for the love of the Lord setteth not by the pleasures of this world, and learneth truly to overcome himself, and with the fervour of spirit crucifieth his flesh, so that in a clean and a pure conscience he may offer his prayers to thee, and be accepted to have company of thy blessed angels, all earthly things excluded from his heart.

Lord, and holy Father, be thou blessed now and ever: for as thou wilt, so is it done, and that thou doest is always best.

Let me, thy humble and unworthy servant, joy only in thee, and not in myself, nor in anything else beside thee.

For thou, Lord, art my gladness, my hope, my crown, and all mine honour.

What hath thy servant but that he hath of thee, and that without his desert?

All things are thine, thou hast created and made them.

I am poor, and have been in trouble and pain ever from my youth, and my soul hath been in great heaviness through manifold passions that come of the world and of the flesh.

Wherefore, Lord, I desire that I may have of thee the joy of inward peace.

I ask of thee to come to that rest, which is ordained for thy chosen children, that are fed and nourished with the light of heavenly comforts, for without thy help I cannot come to thee.

Lord, give me peace, give me inward joy, and then my soul shall be full of heavenly melody, and be devout and fervent in thy lauds and praisings.

But if thou withdraw thyself from me (as thou hast some-time done), then may not thy servant run the way of thy commandments, as I did before.

For it is not with me as it was when the lantern of thy spiritual presence did shine upon my head, and I was defended under the shadow of thy wings from all perils and dangers.

O merciful Lord Jesus, ever to be praised, the time is come that thou wilt prove thy servant, and rightful is it that I shall now suffer somewhat for thee.

Now is the hour come that thou hast known from the beginning, that thy servant for a time should outwardly be set at naught, and inwardly to lean to thee.

And that he should be despised in the sight of the world, and be broken with affliction, that he may after arise with thee in a new light, and be clarified and made glorious in thy kingdom of heaven.

O holy Father, thou hast ordained it so to be, and it is done as thou hast commanded.

This is thy grace, O Lord, to thy friend, to suffer him to be troubled in this world for thy love, how often soever it be, and of what person soever it be, and in what manner soever thou wilt suffer it to fall unto him. For without thy will or sufferance, what thing is done upon earth?

It is good to me, O Lord, that thou hast meekened me, that I may thereby learn to know thy righteous judgments, and to put from me all manner of presumption and stateli-ness of heart.

It is very profitable for me that confusion hath covered my face, that I may learn thereby rather to seek to thee for help and succour than to man.

I have thereby learned to dread thy secret and terrible judgments, which scourgest the righteous with the sinner, but not without equity and justice.

Lord, I yield thanks to thee that thou hast not spared my sins, but hast punished me with scourges of love, and hast sent me affliction and anguish, within and without.

No creature under heaven may comfort me but thou, Lord God, the heavenly surgeon of man's soul, which strikest and healest, who bringest a man nigh unto death, and afterward restorest him to life again, that he may thereby learn to know his own weakness and imbecility and the more fully to trust in thee, Lord.

Thy discipline is laid upon me, and thy rod of correction hath taught me, and under that rod I wholly submit me.

Strike my back and my bones as it shall please thee, and make me to bow my crooked will unto thy will.

Make me a meek and a humble disciple, as thou hast sometime done with me, that I may walk after thy will.

To thee I commit myself to be corrected: for better it is to be corrected by thee here than in time to come.

Thou knowest all things, and nothing is hid from thee that is in man's conscience.

Thou knowest all things to come before they befall, and it is not needful that any man teach thee, or warn thee of any thing that is done upon the earth.

Thou knowest what is profitable for me, and how much tribulations help to purge away the rust of sin in me.

Do with me after thy pleasure; I am a sinful wretch, to none so well known as to thee.

Grant me, Lord, to know that which is necessary to be known: to love that which is to be loved; to desire that which pleaseth thee; to regard that which is precious in thy sight; and to refuse that which is vile before thee.

Suffer me not to judge thy mysteries after my outward senses, nor to give sentence after the hearing of the ignorant, but by true judgment to discern things spiritual, and above all things always to search and follow thy will and pleasure.

O Lord Jesus, thou art all my riches, and all that I have, I have it of thee.

But what am I, Lord, that I dare speak to thee? I am thy poor creature, and a worm most abject.

Behold, Lord, I have naught, and of myself I am naught worth; thou art only God, righteous and holy; thou orderest all things; thou givest all things; and thou fulfillest all things with goodness.

I am a sinner, barren and void of godly virtue.

Remember thy mercies, and fill my heart with plenty of thy grace, for thou wilt not that thy works in me should be made in vain.

How may I bear the misery of this life, except thy grace and mercy do comfort me?

Turn not thy face from me, defer not the visiting of me, withdraw not thy comforts, lest haply my soul be made as dry earth without the water of grace.

Teach me, Lord, to fulfill thy will, to live meekly and worthily before thee, for thou art all my wisdom and cunning, thou art he that knowest me as I am, that knewest me before the world was made, and before I was born or brought into this life. To thee, O Lord, be honour, glory, and praise, for ever and ever. Amen.

Laudes in deum in aeternum.[5]

Amen.

A Prayer for the King

This prayer was rewritten in many forms, specifically mentioning King Henry in the 1545 version, and Edward VI in this version (1547).

5. *Laudes in deum in aeternum*: Praises to the eternal God.

O Lord Jesus Christ, most high, most mighty, King of kings, Lord of lords, the only Ruler of princes, the very Son of God, on whose right hand sitting, dost from thy throne behold all the dwellers upon earth: with most lowly hearts we beseech thee, vouchsafe with favourable regard to behold our most gracious sovereign lord, king Edward the VI, and so replenish him with the grace of thy Holy Spirit, that he always incline to thy will and walk in thy way. Keep him far from ignorance, but through thy gift let prudence and knowledge always abound in his royal heart. So instruct him (O Lord Jesus), reigning upon us in earth, that his human majesty always obey thy divine majesty in fear and dread. Endue him plentifully with heavenly gifts. Grant him in health and wealth long to live. Heap glory and honour upon him. Gladden him with the joy of thy countenance. So strengthen him that he may vanquish and overcome all his and our foes, and be dreaded and feared of all the enemies of his realm.

Amen.

A Prayer for Men to Say Entering into Battle

Almighty King and Lord of hosts, which by thy angels thereunto appointed dost minister both war and peace, and which didst give unto David both courage and strength, being but a little one, unarmed and inexpert in feats of war with his sling to set upon and overthrow the great huge Goliath: our cause now being just and being forced to enter into war and battle, we most humbly beseech thee, O Lord God of Hosts, so to turn the hearts of our enemies to the desire of peace, that no Christian blood be spilt, or else grant, O Lord, that with small effusion of blood, and to the little hurt and damage of innocents, we may to thy glory obtain victory: and that the war's being soon ended, we may all with one heart and mind, knit together in concord and unity, laud and praise thee: which livest and reignest, world without end.

Amen.

A Devout Prayer to Be Daily Said

Almighty and eternal God, which vouchsafest, that we, as it were heavenly children, should every one of us call thee our heavenly Father: Grant, that among us by pureness and example of innocent life, thy most holy name may be sanctified that all other nations, beholding our goodness and virtuous deeds, that thou workest in us, may be stirred to hallow and glorify thee. Grant, O Lord, that the kingdom of thy grace and mercy may reign continually in our hearts, so that we may be worthy, to be partakers of the realm of glory and majesty. Grant, that unto the very death, we refuse not to follow thy divine will, and that we (according to the example of the celestial citizens, agreeing together quietly), united in spirit, all controversy in opinions laid apart, the lusts of the flesh being subdued, and the battering assaults of the world, and the devil overcome, never wrestle against thy most holy will, but obey it in all things. Grant, O Lord, for our body, needful sustenance, that we may the more freely serve thee. Give us, we beseech thee, O merciful Father, that heavenly bread, the body of thy Son Jesus Christ, the very food and health of our souls: give us the bread of thy divine precepts, that we may truly walk and live after them. Give us the bread of thy heavenly word, which is the strong buttress and sure defense of our souls, that we being well fed and filled with this food, may worthily come to the celestial seat where there is no hunger.

Grant, O Lord, that we patiently bear and suffer our enemies, and such as hurt us: and willingly to forgive the offences committed against us: that so we may find thee, Lord, in forgiving us our trespass, mild and merciful. Grant, O Lord, that we be not bitterly led into temptation, that thereby we should be lost: but in all perils of temptation, and in the midst of the stormy tempests of tribulations, let us thy children, perceive and feel thy fatherly succour, ready to help us, lest that we (overcome with the naughty crafts and deception of the tempter) should be drawn into everlasting destruction: but when we be well assayed, approved, and purged with the fire of temptation, then let us finish our course, and so well and valiantly fight, that we may for evermore live with thee, in that heavenly city, where and against the which no manner of temptation can prevail.

Finally, grant, most merciful Father, that we, through thy benign goodness, may be delivered from all evils present and to come, both of body and soul: and that at the last, the yoke of the foul fiend being shaken off, we may possess the heritage of the heavenly kingdom, which thy Son, with his precious blood, bought for us thy children: and there for ever to have the fruition of celestial delectations, accompanied with angels and blessed saints, through the help, benignity, and grace of our Saviour Jesus Christ: to whom, and to thee our Father, and to the Holy Ghost, be glory and honour now and ever,

Amen.

ANOTHER PRAYER

O Heavenly Father, God almighty, I pray and beseech thy mercy, benignly to behold me thy unworthy servant, that I may, by gift of thy Holy Spirit, fervently desire thy kingdom, that I may know thy will, and work thereafter. Give me, O Lord, wisdom: make me constant, patient, and strong in thee. Keep me Lord, from the sleighty[6] invasion of the old wily serpent. Defend me from the counsels and cursings of evil tongues. Let thy mighty arm be my shield against all the malignancy of this wicked world. Remember not, Lord, mine offenses: instruct, prepare me to repent, to be sorry for my sins: make me to love justice and hate wrong, to do good and abstain from all evils: that I may be worthy, to be called thy child. To thee be honour and glory for ever and ever.

Amen.

A Devout Prayer

Lord, hearken to my words. Consider the thought of mine heart. Behold, how loud I cry unto thee. Let my just prayer enter into thine ears, which unfeignedly cometh from mine heart. Hear me, Lord, for I am poor and destitute of man's help. Take care for my soul: save me, thy servant, which wholly trust in thee. Have mercy upon me (O Lord), for I will never cease crying to thee for help.

For thou art mild and more merciful than my tongue can express. As often as adversity assaileth me, I will cry and call for help unto thee. I will call upon thee in the daytime, and in the night my cry shall not be hid from thee. O thou God of the heavens, the Maker of the waters, and Lord of all creatures, hear me, a poor sinner, calling upon thee, and putting my whole trust in thy mercy. Have mercy upon me, O Lord God, have mercy upon me. For thy manifold mercies' sake, forgive all mine offences.

Amen.

6. *Sleighty*: cunning

3

THE PROPHET QUEEN: *THE LAMENTATION OR COMPLAINT OF A SINNER* (1548)

Like the prophet Jeremiah, Katherine weeps over the tragedy of a life of sin. She recalls that "the Prince of princes, the King of kings, did speak many pleasant and gentle words unto me, and also called me so many and sundry times, that they cannot be numbered, and yet, notwithstanding these great signs and tokens of love, I would not come unto him, but hid myself out of his sight, seeking many crooked and by-ways, wherein I walked so long." Katherine, like other Protestants, considered the "crooked and by-ways" to include the teachings of the Roman church.

Although this work is Katherine's confession, her sin is hardly the only matter she takes up. It has an immensely optimistic side. She rejoices in being clothed "in a new garment before God," freed from her sin "and now by his mercy to be taken just and righteous." But she also calls anyone who is swallowed up in sin to confess and lament over his or her guilt. A man or woman should not have "hope nor confidence in any creature, neither in heaven nor earth, but in Christ," his or her "whole and only Saviour."

This edition is taken from the 1548 publication of Katherine's *The Lamentation or Complaint of a Sinner.* The first edition appeared shortly after Henry's death in 1547. Katherine's legendary confrontation with Henry as a result of the conspiracy against her probably prompted her to delay publication. Having passed through many editions, *The Lamentation* was reprinted, updated, and often included in anthologies. This edition of Parr's work is intended to accurately represent the original. A few scattered words that are not found in today's dictionaries are defined in the footnotes. In addition, some spellings, punctuation, paragraphing, and capitalization have been updated. One other modernization tool is the addition of chapter divisions and subheadings; though they did not appear in the original edition, they were added to a later edition and are retained here because they represent a good understanding of the flow of the text.

THE LAMENTATION OR COMPLAINT OF A SINNER,

made by the most virtuous lady Queen Catherine, bewailing the ignorance of her blind life: set forth and put in print at the instant desire of the right gracious lady Catherine duchess of Suffolk, and the earnest request of the right honourable Lord William Parr, Marquess of Northampton.

(Original Preface by William Cecil)

TO THE READER

William Cecil having taken much profit by the reading of this treatise following, wisheth unto every Christian by the reading thereof like profit with increase from God.[1]

1. William Cecil (1520/21–98), the writer of this preface, was the first Baron Burghley. A highly educated man, he attended Cambridge in 1535, and adopted

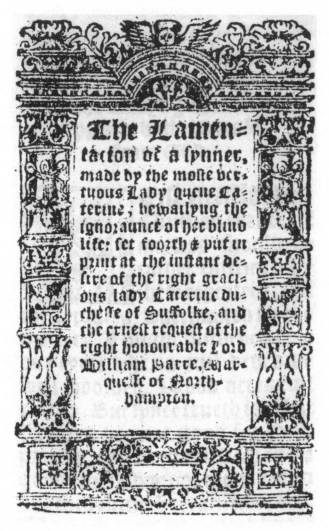

The Lamentacion of a synner, made by the moste vertuous Lady quene Caterine, bewailyng the ignoraunce of her blind life: set foorth & put in prynt at the instant desire of the right gracious lady Caterine duchesse of Suffolke, and the cruest request of the right honourable Lord William Parre, marquesse of Northhampton.

3.1 Title page of *The Lamentation or Complaint of a Sinner* (1548).

Most gentle and Christian reader, if matters should be rather confirmed by their reporters, than the reports warranted by the matters, I might justly bewail our time wherein evil deeds are well worded, and good acts evil cleped.[2] But since truth is that things are not good for their praises, but are praised for their goodness, I do not move thee to like this Christian treatise, because I have mind to praise it, but I exhort thee to mind it, and for the goodness, thou shalt allow it, for whose liking I labour not to obtain, only, moved by my example, their judgment I regard, chiefly confirmed by the matter. Truly, our time is so disposed to grant good names to evil fruits, and excellent terms to mean works, that neither can good deeds enjoy their due names, being defrauded by the evil, neither excellent works can possess their worthy terms, being forestalled by the mean. Insomuch that men seek rather how much they can, than how much they ought to say, inclining more to their pleasure, than to their judgment, and to show themselves rather eloquent, than the matter good, so that neither the goodness of the cause can move them to say more, neither the evilness less. For if the excellency of this Christian contemplation, either for the goodness herein to marvel appearing, either for the profit hereupon to the reader ensuing, should be with due commendation followed, I, of necessity, should either travail to find out new words, the old being anticipated by evil matters, or wish that the common speech of praising were spared, until convenient matters were found to spend it: such is the plenty of praising and scarceness of deserving.

the New Learning ideas of the growing humanism at Cambridge. In the year that *The Lamentation* was first published, Cecil entered into the service of the Lord Protector Somerset. With a few setbacks—once being sent to the Tower of London, and near-death experiences in battle—he moved up in the ranks and was knighted in 1551. Cecil would later help to bring peace with France and Scotland and attempt to bring Reformed polity back into the church.

2. *Cleped*: called.

Wherefore, lacking the manner in words, and not the matter in deed of high commendation, I am compelled to keep in my judgment with silence, trusting that whom my report could not have moved to like this present treatise, the worthiness of the matter shall compel to give it honour.

Any earthly man would soon be stirred to see some mystery of magic, or practice of alchemy, or, perchance, some enchantment of elements: but thou who art christened hast here a wonderful mystery of the mercy of God, a heavenly practice of regeneration, a spiritual enchantment of the grace of God. If joy and triumph be showed when a king's child is born to the world, what joy is sufficient, when God's child is regenerated from heaven. The one is flesh, which is born of flesh: the other is spirit, which is born of Spirit. The one also shall wither like the grass of the earth in short time, the other shall live in heaven beyond all time.

If the finding of one lost sheep be more joyful than the having of ninety and nine, what joy is it to consider the return of a stray child of almighty God, whose return teacheth the ninety and nine to come to their fold? Even such cause of joy is this, that the angels in heaven take comfort herein. Be thou, therefore, joyful when a noble child is newly born: show thyself glad when the lost sheep hath won the whole flock: be thou not sad where angels rejoice.

Here mayest thou see one, if the kind may move thee (a woman), if degree may provoke thee (a woman of high estate), by birth made noble, by marriage most noble, by wisdom godly, by a mighty king, an excellent Queen, by a famous Henry, a renowned Katherine, a wife to him that was a king to realms, refusing the world wherein she was lost, to obtain heaven wherein she may be saved: abhorring sin, which made her bound, to receive grace, whereby she may be free: despising flesh, the cause of corruption, to put on the Spirit, the cause of sanctification: forsaking ignorance, wherein she was blind, to come to knowledge, whereby she may see: removing superstition, wherewith she was smothered, to embrace true religion, wherewith she may revive.

The fruit of this treatise, good reader, is thy amendment: this only had, the writer is satisfied. This good lady thought no shame to detest her sin to obtain remission: no vileness, to become nothing, to be a member of him which is all things in all: no folly to forget the wisdom of the world, to learn the simplicity of the gospel: at the last, no displeasantness to submit herself to the school of the cross, the learning of the crucifix, the book of our redemption, the very absolute library of God's mercy and wisdom. This way, thought she, her honour increased, and her state permanent, to make her earthly honour heavenly, and neglect the transitory for the everlasting.

Of this I would have thee warned, that the profit may ensue. These great mysteries and graces are not well perceived, except they are surely studied, neither are they perfectly studied, except they are diligently practised: neither profitably practised, without amendment. See and learn hereby what she hath done, then mayest thou practise and amend that thou canst do: so shalt thou practise with ease, having a guide, and amend with profit, having a zeal. It is easier to see these, than to learn: begin at the easiest to come to the harder: see thou her confession, that thou mayest learn her repentance: practise her perseverance, that thou mayest have like amendment: despise thyself in eschewing vice, that thou mayest please God in asking grace: let not shame hinder thy confession, which hindered not the offence. Be thou sure, "if we acknowledge our sins, God is faithful to forgive us, and to cleanse us from all unrighteousness" [1 John 1:9]. Obey the prophet's saying, declare thy ways to the Lord.

Thus far thou mayest learn to know thyself: next this, be thou as diligent to relieve thyself in God's mercy, as ye hast been to reveal thyself in thine own repentance. For God hath concluded all things under sin, because he would have mercy upon all, who hath also borne our sins in his body upon the tree, that we should be delivered from sin, and should live unto righteousness, by whose stripes we are healed. Here is our anchor, here is our shepherd, here we are made whole, here is our life, our redemption, our salvation, and our bliss: let us therefore now feed by this gracious Queen's example, and be not ashamed to become in confession publicans, since this noble lady will be no Pharisee.

And to all ladies of estate I wish as earnest mind to follow our Queen in virtue, as in honour, that they might once appear to prefer God before the world: and be honourable in religion, who now are honourable in vanities: so shall they (as in some virtuous ladies of right high estate it is with great comfort seen) taste of this freedom, of remission, of the everlasting bliss, which exceeds all thoughts and understandings, and is prepared for the holy in spirit, for the which let us with our intercession in holiness and pureness of life, offer ourselves to the heavenly Father an undefiled host: to whom be eternal praise and glory, through all the earth, without end. Amen.

Chapter One

Of an humble confession of sins to the glory of God

When I consider, in the bethinking of mine evil and wretched former life, mine obstinate, stony, and untractable[3] heart to have so much exceeded in evilness, that it hath not only neglected, yea contemned, and despised God's

3. *Untractable*: obstinate.

holy precepts and commandments: but also embraced, received, and esteemed vain, foolish, and feigned trifles: I am partly by the hate I owe to sin, who hath reigned in me, partly by the love I owe to all Christians, whom I am content to edify, even with the example of mine own shame, forced and constrained with my heart and words, to confess and declare to the world, how ingrate, negligent, unkind, and stubborn, I have been to God my Creator: and how beneficial, merciful, and gentle, he hath been always to me his creature, being such a miserable and wretched sinner.

Truly I have taken no little small thing upon me, first to set forth my whole stubbornness and contempt in words the which is incomprehensible in thought (as it is in the Psalm), "Who understandeth his faults?" [Ps. 19:12]. Next this, to declare the excellent beneficence, mercy, and goodness of God, which is infinite and unmeasurable. Neither can all the words of angels and men make relation thereof, as appertaineth to his most high goodness. Who is he that is not forced to confess the same, if he consider what he hath received of God, and doth daily receive? Yea if men would not acknowledge and confess the same, the stones would cry it out [Luke 19:40]. Truly I am constrained and forced to speak and write thereof to mine own confusion and shame, but to the glory and praise of God. For he as a loving Father, of most abundant and high goodness, hath heaped upon me innumerable benefits. And I, contrary, have heaped manifold sins, despising that which was good, holy, pleasant, and acceptable in his sight, and choosing that which was delicious, pleasant, and acceptable in my sight.

And no marvel it was that I so did, for I would not learn to know the Lord and his ways, but loved darkness better than light, yea darkness seemed to me light [John 1:3]. I embraced ignorance as perfect knowledge, and knowledge seemed to me superfluous and vain. I regarded little God's word, but gave myself to vanities and shadows of the world. I forsook him, in whom is all truth, and followed the vain, foolish imaginations of my heart. I would have covered my sins with the pretence of holiness, I called superstition godly meaning, and true holiness error. The Lord did speak many pleasant and sweet words unto me, and I would not hear. He called me diversely, but through frowardness I would not answer.

Mine evils and miseries are so many and great, that they accuse me even to my face. Oh, how miserably and wretchedly am I confounded, when for the multitude and greatness of my sins I am compelled to accuse myself. Was it not a marvelous unkindness when God did speak to me, and also call me, that I would not answer him? What man, so called, would not have heard? Or what man, hearing, would not have answered? If an earthly prince had spoken, either called him, I suppose there be none, but would willingly have done both. Now therefore what a wretch and caitiff[4] am I? That when the Prince of princes, the King of kings, did speak many pleasant and gentle words unto me, and also called me so many and sundry times, that they cannot be numbered, and yet, notwithstanding these great signs and tokens of love, I would not come unto him, but hid myself out of his sight, seeking many crooked and by-ways, wherein I walked so long that I had clean lost his sight. And no marvel or wonder, for I had a blind guide called Ignorance, who dimmed so mine eyes, that I could never perfectly get any sight of the fair, goodly, straight, and right ways of his doctrine: but continually traveled uncomfortably, in foul, wicked, crooked, and perverse ways. Yea, and because they were so much haunted of many, I could not think but I walked in the perfect and right way, having more regard to the number of the walkers, than to the order of

4. *Caitiff*: miserable person or captive.

the walking: believing also, most surely with company to have walked to heaven, whereas I am most sure they would have brought me down to hell.

I forsook the spiritual honouring of the true living God, and worshiped visible idols, and images made of men's hands, believing by them to have gotten heaven, yea to say the truth I made a great idol of myself, for I loved myself better than God. And certainly look how many things are loved or preferred in our hearts before God, so many are taken and esteemed for idols, and false gods.

Alas, how have I violated this holy, pure, and most high precept and commandment of the love of God? Which precept bindeth me to love him with my whole heart, mind, force, strength, and understanding [Deut. 6:5]. And I like unto an evil, wicked, and disobedient child, have given my will, power, and senses to the contrary: making almost of every earthly and carnal thing a god. Furthermore, the blood of Christ was not reputed by me sufficient for to wash me from the filth of my sins: neither such ways as he hath appointed by his word. But I sought for such riffraff as the bishop of Rome hath planted in his tyranny and kingdom, trusting with great confidence by the virtue and holiness of them, to receive full remission of my sins. And so I did as much as was in me to obfuscate and darken the great benefit of Christ's passion, than the which no thought can conceive anything of more value. There cannot be done so great an injury and displeasure to almighty God, our Father, as to tread under foot Christ, his only begotten and well-beloved Son. All other sins in the world, gathered together in one, are not so heinous and detestable in the sight of God. And no wonder, for in Christ crucified, God doth show himself most noble and glorious, even an almighty God, and most loving Father, in his only dear and chosen blessed Son.

And therefore I count myself one of the most wicked and miserable sinners, because I have been so much contrary to Christ my Saviour. St. Paul desired to know nothing, but Christ crucified [1 Cor. 2:2] after he had been rapt into the third heaven, where he heard such secrets as were not convenient and meet to utter to men, but counted all his works and doings as nothing, to win Christ [Phil. 3:7].

And I, most presumptuously thinking nothing of Christ crucified, went about to set forth mine own righteousness, saying with the proud Pharisee, "Good Lord, I thank thee, I am not like other men. I am none adulterer, nor fornicator," and so forth [Luke 18:11], with such like words of vainglory, extolling myself, and despising others, working as an hired servant for wages, or else for reward: and not as a loving child, only for very love, without respect of wages or reward, as I ought to have done. Neither did I consider how beneficial a Father I had, who did show me his charity and mercy of his own mere grace and goodness, that when I was most his enemy [Rom. 5:10], he sent his only begotten and well-beloved Son into this world of wretchedness and misery, to suffer most cruel and sharp death for my redemption. But my heart was so stony and hard, that this great benefit was never truly and lively printed in my heart, although with my words it was oft rehearsed, thinking myself to be sufficiently instructed in the same, and being indeed in blind ignorance. And yet I stood so well in mine own judgment and opinion that I thought it vain to seek the increase of my knowledge therein.

Paul calleth Christ the wisdom of God [1 Cor. 1:24], and even the same Christ, was to me foolishness. My pride and blindness deceived me, and the hardness of my heart withstood the growing of truth within it. Such were the fruits of my carnal and human reason—to have rotten ignorance in price for ripe and seasonable knowledge. Such also is the malice and wickedness that possesseth the hearts of men; such is the wisdom and pleasing of the flesh. I professed Christ in my baptism when I began to live, but I swerved from him after baptism, in continuance of my living, even as the heathen, which never had begun.

Christ was innocent and void of all sin, and I wallowed in filthy sin, and was free from no sin. Christ was obedient unto his Father, even to the death of the cross [Phil. 2:8], and I disobedient, and most stubborn, even to the confusion of truth. Christ was meek and humble in heart [Matt. 5], and I most proud and vainglorious. Christ despised the world [Matt. 4] with all the vanities thereof, and I made it my god because of the vanities. Christ came to serve his brethren [John 13], and I coveted to rule over them.[5] Christ despised worldly honour, and I much delighted to attain the same. Christ loved the base and simple things of the world and I esteemed the most fair and pleasant things. Christ loved poverty [2 Cor. 8:9], and I wealth. Christ was gentle and merciful to the poor [Luke 14:12], and I hard hearted and ungentle. Christ prayed for his enemies [Luke 23:34], and I hated mine. Christ rejoiced in the conversion of sinners [Matt. 9:35ff], and I was not grieved to see their reversion to sin. By this declaration all creatures may perceive how far I was from Christ, and without Christ, yea, how contrary to Christ, although I bare the name of a Christian. Insomuch that if any man had said I had been

5. According to a possibly apocryphal story from John Strype, Katherine's parents were told by an astrologer in her infancy that she would one day rise to power, saying that "she was born to sit in the highest seat of imperial majesty, having all the eminent stars and planets in her house." It was said that when she was called to work by her mother, she would reply, "My hands are ordained to touch crowns and scepters, not needles and spindles." (John Strype, *Ecclesiastical Memorials Relating Chiefly to Religion and the Reformation of It and the Emergencies of the Church of England under King Henry VIII, King Edward VI, and Queen Mary I with Large Appendixes, Containing Original Papers, Records, &c*, vol. 2.1 [Oxford: Clarendon Press, 1822], 206.)

without Christ, I would have stiffly withstood the same. And yet I neither knew Christ, nor wherefore he came.

As concerning the effect and purpose of his coming, I had a certain vain blind knowledge, both cold and dead, which may be had with all sin [Rom. 2], as doth plainly appear by this my confession and open declaration.

Chapter Two

Repentance in faith and Christ's merits

What cause now have I to lament, sigh, and weep for my life and time so evil spent? With how much humility and lowliness ought I to come and acknowledge my sins to God; giving him thanks, that it hath pleased him of his abundant goodness to give me time of repentance. For I know my sins, in the consideration of them, to be so grievous, and in the number so exceeding, that I have deserved very often eternal damnation. And for the deserving of God's wrath, so manifoldly due, I must incessantly give thanks to the mercy of God, beseeching also that the same delay of punishment cause not his plague to be the sorer, since mine own conscience condemns my former doings. But his mercy exceedeth all iniquity [Ps. 103:3]. And if I should not thus hope, alas what should I seek for refuge and comfort? No mortal man is of power to help me [Ps. 108:12]: and for the multitude of my sins, I dare not lift up mine eyes to heaven where the seat of judgment is, I have so much offended God. What shall I fall in desperation? Nay I will call upon Christ the Light of the world [1 John 1:5–7], the fountain of life, the relief of all careful, and the peacemaker between God and man [1 John 2:1–2], and the only health and comfort of all true repentant sinners [John 3].

He can by his almighty power save me and deliver me out of this miserable state, and hath will by his mercy to save even the whole sin of the world [John 3:16; 1 John 2:1]. I have no hope nor confidence in any creature, neither in heaven nor earth, but in Christ my whole and only Saviour. He came into the world to save sinners [Matt. 1:21], and to heal them that are sick, for he said, the whole have no need of a physician. Behold Lord, how I come to thee, a sinner, sick, and grievously wounded. I ask not bread, but the crumbs that fall from the children's table. Cast me not out of thy sight, although I have deserved to be cast into hell fire.

If I should look upon my sins, and not upon thy mercy I should despair: for in myself I find nothing to save me, but a dunghill of wickedness to condemn me. If I should hope by mine own strength and power to come out of this maze of iniquity and wickedness, wherein I have walked so long, I should be deceived. For I am so ignorant, blind, weak, and feeble that I cannot bring myself out of this entangled and wayward maze: but the more I seek means and ways to wind myself out, the more I am wrapped and tangled therein.

So that I perceive my striving therein to be hindrance, my travail to be labour spent in going back. It is the hand of the Lord that can and will bring me out of this endless maze of death. For without I be prevented by the grace of the Lord, I cannot ask forgiveness nor be repentant or sorry for them. There is no man can avow that Christ is the only Saviour of the world, but by the Holy Ghost [1 Cor. 2]: yea as St. Paul saith, no man can say "the Lord Jesus" but by the Holy Ghost. The Spirit helpeth our infirmity, and maketh continual intercession for us, with such sorrowful groanings as cannot be expressed [Rom. 8:26].

Therefore I will first require and pray the Lord, to give me his Holy Spirit to teach me to avow that Christ is the

Saviour of the world, and to utter these words, "The Lord Jesus," and finally to help mine infirmities, and to intercede for me. For I am most certain and sure, that no creature in heaven nor earth is of power, or can by any mean help me, but God, who is omnipotent, almighty, beneficial, and merciful, wellwilling, and loving to all those that call and put their whole confidence and trust in him [Acts 4:12]. And therefore, I will seek no other means, nor advocate, but Christ's Holy Spirit, who is only the advocate and mediator between God and man, to help and relieve me.

Chapter Three

What true faith works in the soul of a sinner

But now what maketh me so bold and hardy, to presume to come to the Lord with such audacity and boldness being so great a sinner? Truly nothing but his own word. For he saith, "Come to me, all ye that labour, and are burdened, and I shall refresh you" [Matt. 11:28]. What gentle, merciful, and comfortable words are these to all sinners? Were he not a frantic, mad, beastly, and foolish man, that would run for aid, helps, or refuge to any other creature? What a most gracious, comfortable, and gentle saying was this, with such pleasant and sweet words, to allure his enemies to come unto him? Is there any worldly prince or magistrate, that would show such clemency and mercy to their disobedient and rebellious subjects, having offended them? I suppose they would not with such words allure them except it were to call those whom they cannot take, and punish them being taken. But even as Christ is Prince of princes, and Lord of lords, so his charity and mercy exceedeth and surmounteth all others. Christ saith, "If carnal fathers do give good gifts to their children when they ask them, how much more shall your heavenly Father, being in substance all holy, and most highly good, give good gifts to all them that ask him?" [Matt. 7:11].

It is no small nor little gift that I now require, neither think I myself worthy to receive such a noble gift, being so ingrate, unkind, and wicked a child. But when I behold the benignity, liberality, mercy, and goodness of the Lord, I am encouraged, boldened, and stirred to ask such a noble gift. The Lord is so bountiful and liberal, that he will not have us satisfied and contented with one gift, neither to ask simple and small gifts. And therefore he promiseth and bindeth himself by his word, to give good and beneficial gifts to all them that ask him with true faith [John 16:23–24], without which nothing can be done acceptable or pleasing to God [Rom. 8:8]. For faith is the foundation and ground of all other gifts, virtues, and graces; and therefore I will say, Lord, increase my faith.

For this is the life everlasting, Lord, that I must believe thee to be the true God, and who thou didst send, Jesus Christ [1 John 4]. By this faith I am assured, and by this assurance I feel the remission of my sins. This is it that maketh me bold, this is it that comforteth me, this is it that quencheth all despair.

I know, O my Lord, thy eyes look upon my faith. St. Paul saith, "we are justified by the faith in Christ, and not by the deeds of the law; for if righteousness come by the law, then Christ died in vain" [Rom. 5; Gal. 2:21; Eph. 2:8–9]. St. Paul meaneth not here a dead, human, historical faith, gotten by human industry, but a supernatural, lively faith, which worketh by charity, as he himself plainly expresses. This dignity of faith is no derogation to good works; for out of this faith spring all good works. Yet we may not impute to the worthiness of faith or works our justification before God, but ascribe and give the worthiness of it wholly to the merits of Christ's passion, and refer and attribute the knowledge and perceiving thereof only to faith: whose very true only property is to take, apprehend, and hold fast the promises of God's mercy, the which maketh us righteous: and to cause me continually to hope for the same mercy, and in love to work all manner of ways allowed in the scripture, that I may be thankful for the same.

Thus I feel myself to come, as it were, in a new garment before God; and now by his mercy to be taken just and righteous, which of late without his mercy, was sinful and wicked; and by faith to obtain his mercy, the which the unfaithful cannot enjoy. And although St. John extolleth charity in his epistle, saying that "God is charity, and he that dwelleth in charity dwelleth in God" [1 John 4:7–8]. Truly, charity maketh men live like angels, and of the most furious, unbridled, carnal men, maketh meek lambs.

Yea, with how fervent a spirit ought I to call, cry, and pray to the Lord to make his great charity to burn and flame my heart, being stony and evil affected, that it never would conceive nor regard the great inestimable charity and love of God, in sending his only begotten and dear beloved Son into this vale of misery to suffer the most cruel and sharp death of the cross for my redemption. Yet I never had this unspeakable and most high charity and abundant love of God printed and fixed in my heart duly, till it pleased God of his mere grace, mercy, and pity, to open mine eyes, making me to see and behold with the eye of lively faith, Christ crucified to be mine only Saviour and Redeemer. For then I began (and not before) to perceive and see mine own ignorance and blindness; the cause thereof was that I would not learn to know Christ my Saviour and Redeemer.

But when God of his mere goodness had thus opened mine eyes, and made me see and behold Christ, the Wisdom of God, the Light of the world, with a supernatural sight of faith [1 Cor. 2:14], all pleasures, vanities, honour, riches, wealth, and aids of the world began to wax bitter unto me. Then I knew it was no illusion of the devil, nor false, nor human doctrine I had received. When such success came thereof, that I had in detestation and horror that which I erst so much loved and esteemed, being of God forbidden that we should love the world [1 John 2:15] or the vain pleasures and shadows in the same, then began I to perceive that Christ was my only Saviour and Redeemer, and the same doctrine to be all divine, holy, and heavenly, infused by grace into the hearts of the faithful, which never can be attained by human doctrine, wit, nor reason, although they should travail and labour for the same to the end of the world. Then began I to dwell in God by charity, knowing, by the loving charity of God in the remission of my sins, that God is charity, as St. John saith [1 John 4:7–8]. So that of my faith (whereby I came to know God, and whereby it pleased God, even because I trusted in him, to justify me) sprang this excellent charity in my heart.

I think no less, but many will wonder and marvel at this my saying, that I never knew Christ for my Saviour and Redeemer until this time. For many have this opinion, saying, Who knoweth not there is a Christ? Who being a Christian doth not confess him his Saviour? And thus believing their dead, human, historical faith and knowledge (which they have learned in their scholastical books) to be the true infused faith and knowledge of Christ, which may be had (as I said before) with all sin, they used to say, by their own experience of themselves, that their faith doth not justify them. And true it is, except they have this faith the which I have declared here before, they shall never be justified.

And yet it is not false that by faith only[6] I am sure to be justified. Even this is the cause that so many impugn this

6. *Faith only*: Here she refers to the Protestant slogan, *sola fide*.

office and duty of true faith, because so many lack the true faith. And even as the faithful are forced to allow true faith, so the unfaithful can in no wise probably entreat thereof: the one feeling in himself that [which] he saith, the other having not in him for to say.

I have certainly no curious learning to defend this matter withal, but a simple zeal and earnest love to the truth inspired of God, who promiseth to pour his Spirit upon all flesh, which I have by the grace of God (whom I most humbly honour) felt in myself to be true.

Chapter Four

God's love for humanity and Christ crucified

Let us therefore now, I pray you, by faith behold and consider the great charity and goodness of God in sending his Son to suffer death for our redemption, when we were his mortal enemies, and after what sort and manner he sent him.

First it is to be considered, yea to be undoubtedly with a perfect faith believed, that God sent him to us freely, for he did give him and sold him not. A more noble and rich gift he could not have given. He sent not a servant or a friend, but his only Son [John 3:16], so dearly beloved: not in delights, riches, and honours, but in crosses, poverties, and slanders: not as a lord but as a servant [Phil. 2:7], yea and in most vile and painful passions to wash us not with water but with his own precious blood, not from mire but from the puddle and filth of our iniquities. He hath given him not to make us poor, but to enrich us with his divine virtues, merits, and graces, yea and in him he hath given us all good things, and finally himself, and that with such great charity as cannot be expressed.

Was it not a most high and abundant charity of God to send Christ to shed his blood, to lose honour, life, and all for his enemies [Rom. 5:6–8]? Even in the time when we had done him most injury he first showed his charity to us with such flames of love that greater could not be showed. God in Christ hath opened unto us (although we are weak and blind of ourselves) that we may behold in this miserable estate the great wisdom, goodness, and truth, with all the other godly perfections which are in Christ. Therefore inwardly to behold Christ crucified upon the cross is the best and godliest meditation that can be. We may see also in Christ crucified, the beauty of the soul better than in all the books of the world.

For who that with lively faith seeth and feeleth in spirit that Christ, the Son of God, is dead for the satisfying and purifying of the soul, shall see that his soul is appointed for the very tabernacle and mansion of the inestimable and incomprehensible majesty and honour of God [John 4]. We see also in Christ crucified how vain and foolish the world is, and how that Christ, being most wise, despised the same. We see also how blind it is, because the same knoweth not Christ, but persecuteth him. We see also how unkind the world is, by the killing of Christ, in the time he did show it most favour. How hard and obstinate was it that would not be mollified with so many tears? Such sweat, and so much bloodshed of the Son of God, suffering with so great and high charity?

Therefore he is now very blind that seeth not how vain, foolish, false, ingrate, cruel, hard, wicked, and evil the world is. We may also in Christ crucified weigh our sins, as in a divine balance, how grievous and how weighty they are, seeing they have crucified Christ; for they would never have been counterpayed but with the great and precious weight of the blood of the Son of God. And therefore God of his high goodness, determined that his blessed Son should rather suffer bloodshed than our sins should have condemned us. We shall never know our own misery and wretchedness but with the light of Christ crucified. Then we shall see our own cruelty, when we feel his mercy, our own unrighteousness and iniquity, when we see his righteousness and holiness. Therefore, to learn to know truly our own sins is to study in the book of the crucifix, by continual conversation in faith: and to have perfect and plentiful charity is to learn first by faith the charity that is in God towards us.

We may see also in Christ upon the cross how great the pains of hell, and how blessed the joys of heaven, be: and what a sharp, painful thing it shall be to them that from that sweet, happy, and glorious joy, Christ, shall be deprived. Then this crucifix is the book wherein God hath included all things, and hath most compendiously written therein all truth profitable and necessary for our salvation [1 Cor. 2]. Therefore let us endeavour ourselves to study this book, that we, being enlightened with the Spirit of God, may give him thanks for so great a benefit.

Chapter Five

Christ's glorious victories over all enemies

If we look further in this book, we shall see Christ's great victory upon the cross, which was so noble and mighty that there never was, neither shall be such. If the victory and glory of worldly princes were great because they did overcome great hosts of men, how much more was Christ's greater, which vanquished not only the prince of this world, but all the enemies of God: triumphing over persecution, injuries, villainies, slanders, yea death, the world, sin, and the devil, and brought to confusion all carnal prudence.

The princes of the world never did fight without the strength of the world. Christ contrarily went to war even against all the strength of the world. He would fight as David did with Goliath [1 Sam. 17], unarmed of all human wisdom and policy, and without all worldly power and strength. Nevertheless he was fully replenished and armed with the whole armour of the Spirit. And in this one battle he overcame forever, all his enemies.

There was never so glorious a spoil, neither a more rich and noble, than Christ was upon the cross, who delivered all his elect from such a sharp miserable captivity. He had in this battle many stripes, yea, and lost his life, but his victory was so much the greater. Therefore when I look upon the Son of God with a supernatural faith and sight, so unarmed, naked, given up, and alone with humility, patience, liberality, modesty, gentleness, and with all other his divine virtues, beating down to the ground all God's enemies, and making the soul of man so fair and beautiful, I am forced to say that his victory and triumph was marvelous. And therefore Christ deserved to have this noble title, Jesus of Nazareth, King of the Jews [Matt. 27:37].

But if we will particularly unfold and see his great victories, let us first behold how he overcame sin with his innocency, and confounded pride with his humility, quenched all worldly love with his charity, appeased the wrath of his Father with his meekness, turned hatred into love with his so many benefits and godly zeal.

Christ hath not only overcome sin, but rather he hath killed the same: inasmuch as he hath satisfied for it himself with the most holy sacrifice and oblation of his precious body in suffering most bitter and cruel death. Also after another sort, that is, he giveth all those that love him so much spirit, grace, virtue, and strength, that they may resist, impugn, and overcome sin, and not consent, neither suffer it to reign in them [Rom. 6–7]. He hath also vanquished sin because he hath taken away the force of the same: that is, he hath canceled the law, which was in evil men the occasion of sin [Col. 2:11–14]. Therefore sin hath no power against them that are, with the Holy Ghost, united to Christ. In them there is nothing worthy of damnation. And although the dregs of Adam do remain, that is our concupiscences, which indeed be sins: nevertheless they are not imputed for sins, if we be truly planted in Christ [Rom. 8:1–2]. It is true that Christ might have taken away all our immoderate affections, but he hath left them for the greater glory of his Father, and for his own greater triumph. As for an example: when a prince fights with his enemies, which sometime had the sovereignty over his people, and subduing them, may kill them if he will, yet he preserves and saves them, and whereas they were lords over his people, he makes them after to serve whom they before had ruled.

Now in such a case, the prince does show himself a greater conqueror, in that he hath made them which were rulers to obey: and the subjects to be lords over them to whom they served, than if he had utterly destroyed them upon the conquest. For now he leaves continual victory to them whom he redeemed, whereas otherwise the occasion of victory was taken away where none were left to be the subjects. Even so in like case, Christ hath left in us these concupiscences, to the intent they should serve us to the exercise of our virtues, where first they did reign over us to the exercise of our sin. And it may be plainly seen, that whereas first they were such impediments to us that we could not move ourselves towards God, now by Christ we have so much strength, that notwithstanding the force of them, we may assuredly walk to heaven. And although the children of God sometime do fall by frailty into some sin, yet that falling maketh them to humble themselves, and to acknowledge the goodness of God, and to come to him for refuge and help.

Likewise Christ, with his death, hath overcome the prince of devils with all his host, and hath destroyed them all. For, as Paul saith, this is verified that Christ should break the serpent's head, prophesied by God [Rom. 16:20]. And although the devil tempt us [Gen. 3], yet if by faith we are planted in Christ, we shall not perish, but rather by his temptation take great force and might. So it is evident that the triumph, victory, and glory of Christ is the greater, having in such sort subdued the devil, that whereas he was prince and lord of the world, holding all creatures in captivity, now Christ useth him as an instrument to punish the wicked, and to exercise and make strong the elect of God, in Christian warfare.

Christ likewise hath overcome death in a more glorious manner (if it be possible), because he hath not taken it away, but leaving universally all subject to the same. He hath given so much virtue and spirit, that whereas afore we passed thereto with great fear, now we are bold through the Spirit, for the sure hope of resurrection, that we receive it with joy. It is now no more bitter, but sweet; no more feared, but desired; it is no death, but life.

And also it hath pleased God that the infirmities and adversities do remain to the sight of the world: but the children of God are by Christ made so strong, righteous, whole, and sound, that the troubles of the world are comforts of the spirit [Phil. 4:6–9], the passions of the flesh are medicines of the soul. For all manner of things work to their commodity and profit [Rom. 8:28]. For they in spirit feel that God their Father doth govern them, and disposeth all things for their benefit; therefore they feel themselves sure. In persecution they are quiet and peaceful: in time of trouble, they are without weariness, fears, anxieties, suspicions, miseries, and finally, all the good and evil of the world worketh to their commodity.

Moreover, they see that the triumph of Christ hath been so great, that not only he hath subdued and vanquished all our enemies and the power of them, but he hath overthrown and vanquished them after such a sort, that all things serve to our health. He might and could have taken them all away, but where then should have been our victory, palm, and crown? For we daily have fights in the flesh, and by the succour of grace have continual victories over sin, whereby we have cause to glorify God who, by his Son, hath weakened our enemy the devil, and by his Spirit giveth us strength to vanquish his offsprings.

So do we acknowledge daily the great triumph of our Saviour, and rejoice in our own fights, the which we can no wise impute to any wisdom of this world, seeing sin to increase by it. And where worldly wisdom most governeth, there most sin ruleth; for as the world is enemy to God, so also the wisdom thereof is adverse to God. And therefore Christ hath declared and discovered the same for foolishness [1 Cor. 1:20–21]. And although he could have taken away all worldly wisdom, yet he hath left it for his greater glory and triumph of his chosen vessels. For before, whereas it was our ruler against God, now by Christ we are served of it for God, as of a slave in worldly things.

Albeit in supernatural things the same is not to be understood. And further if any time men would impugn and gainsay us with the wisdom of the world, yet we have by Christ, so much supernatural light of the truth, that we make a mock of all those that repugn the truth. Christ also upon the cross, hath triumphed over the world. First, because he hath discovered the same to be naught, and whereas it was covered with the veil of hypocrisy, and the vesture of moral virtues, Christ hath showed that in God's sight, the righteousness of the world is wickedness: and he hath yielded witness, that the works of men, not regenerated by him in faith, are evil. And so Christ hath judged and condemned the world for naught. Furthermore he hath given to all his so much light and spirit, that they know it and dispraise the same: yea and tread it under their feet, with all vain honours, dignities, and pleasures, not taking the fair promises, neither the offers which it doth present. Nay they rather make a scorn of them. And as for the threatenings and force of the world, they nothing fear.

Now therefore we may see how great the victory and triumph of Christ is, who hath delivered all those the Father gave him from the power of the devil [John 17:12], canceling upon the cross the writing of our debts: for he hath delivered us from the condemnation of sin, from the bondage of the law, from the fear of death, from the danger of the world, and from all evils in this life and in the other to come. And he hath enriched us, made us noble, and most highly happy, after such a glorious and triumphant way as cannot with tongue be expressed. And therefore we are forced to say his triumph is marvelous.

It is also seen and known that Christ is the true Messiah, for he hath delivered man from all evils, and by him man hath all goodness, so that he is the true Messiah. Therefore all other helpers are but vain and counterfeited Saviours, seeing that by this our Messiah Christ, wholly and only, we are delivered from all evils, and by him we have all goodness. And that this is true, it is evident and clear, because the very true Christian is a Christian by Christ. And the true Christian feeleth inwardly by Christ, so much goodness of God, that even troublous life and death are sweet unto him, and miseries happy. The true Christian by Christ, is disburdened from the servitude of the law, having the law of grace (graven by the Spirit) inhabiting his heart, and from sin that reigned in him, from the power of the infernal spirits, from damnation, and from every evil: and is made a son of God, a brother of Christ, heir of heaven, and lord of the world. So that in Christ and by Christ, he possesses all good things [Rom. 6–7].

But let us know that Christ yet fighteth in spirit in his elect vessels, and shall fight even to the day of judgment, at which day shall that great enemy death, be wholly destroyed, and shall be no more. Then shall the children of God rejoice in him, saying: O death, where is thy victory and sting? There shall be then no more trouble nor sin, nay rather, none evil, but heaven for the good, and hell for the wicked. Then shall wholly be discovered the victory and triumph of Christ, who (after Paul) shall present unto his Father the kingdom, together with his chosen saved by him [1 Cor. 15:24].

It was no little favor towards his children, that Christ was chosen of God to save us, his elect, so highly by the way of the cross. Paul calleth it a grace, and a most singular grace. We may well think, that he, having been to the world so valiant a captain of God, was full of light, grace, virtue, and spirit, therefore he might justly say [John 19:30]: *consummatum est* ["It is finished"]. We seeing then that the triumph and victory of our Captain Christ is so marvelous, glorious, and noble, to the which war we are appointed, let us force ourselves to follow him, with bearing our cross, that we may have fellowship with him in his kingdom.

Chapter Six

On submission to the cross and Scripture

Truly it may be most justly verified that to behold Christ crucified, in spirit, is the best meditation that can be. I certainly never knew mine own miseries and wretchedness so well by book, admonition, or learning, as I have done by looking into the spiritual book of the crucifix. I lament much I have passed so many years not regarding that divine book, but I judged and thought myself to be well instructed in the same: whereas now I am of this opinion, that if God would suffer me to live here a thousand years, and should study continually in the same divine book, I should not be filled with the contemplation thereof. Neither hold I myself contented, but always have a great desire to learn and study more therein. I never knew mine own wickedness, neither lamented for my sins truly, until the time God inspired me with his grace, that I looked in this book. Then I began to see perfectly that mine own power and strength could not help me, and that I was in the Lord's hand, even as the clay is in the potter's hand [Jer. 18:6; Rom. 9:21–23]: then I began to cry and say: "Alas! Lord, that ever I have so wickedly offended thee, being to me, from the beginning, so gracious, and so good a Father, and, most specially, now hast declared and showed thy goodness unto me, when in the time I have done thee most injury, to call me, and also to make me know, and take thee for my Savior and Redeemer."

Such be the wonderful works of God, to call sinners to repentance, and to make them to take Christ, his well-beloved Son, for their Savior: this is the gift of God, and of all Christians to be required and desired. For except this great benefit of Christ crucified be felt and fixed surely in man's heart, there can be no good work done acceptable before God. For in Christ is all fullness of the Godhead [Col. 2:9], and in him are hid all the treasures of wisdom and knowledge: even he is the water of life, whereof whosoever shall drink, he shall never more thirst, but it shall be in him a well of water, springing up into everlasting life [John 4:14]. St. Paul saith, "there is no damnation to them that are in Christ, which walk not after the flesh, but after the Spirit" [Rom. 8:1]. Moreover he saith, "if, when we were enemies, we were reconciled to God, by the death of his Son, much more, seeing we are reconciled, we shall be preserved by his life" [Rom. 5:10].[7] It is no little or small benefit we have received by Christ, if we consider what he hath done for us, as I have perfectly declared heretofore. Wherefore I pray the Lord that this great benefit of Christ crucified may be steadfastly fixed and printed in all Christian hearts, that they may be true lovers of God, and work as children, for love: and not as servants, compelled with threatenings or provoked with hire.

The sincere and pure lovers of God do embrace Christ with such fervency of spirit, that they rejoice in hope, are bold in danger, suffer in adversity, continue in prayer, bless their persecutors. Further they are not wise in their own opinion, neither high-minded in their prosperity, neither abashed in their adversity, but humble and gentle always to all men. For they know by their faith they are members all of one body, and that they have possessed all one God, one faith, one baptism, one joy, and one salvation [Eph. 4:4–6]. If these pure and sincere lovers of God were thickly sown, there should not be so much contention and strife growing on the fields of our religion as there is. Well I shall pray to the Lord to take all contention and strife away, and that the sowers of sedition may have mind to cease their labor, or to sow it among the stones, and to have grace to sow gracious virtues, where they may both root and bring forth fruit, with sending also a godly unity and concord amongst all Christians, that we may serve the Lord in true holiness of life.

7. *Preserved by his life*: This has been corrected from the original, which read "preserved by his death."

Chapter Seven

On lamenting the miserable ignorance and blindness of humanity

The example of good living is required of all Christians, but especially in the ecclesiastical pastors and shepherds. For they are called in scripture, workmen with God [1 Cor. 3:9], disbursers of God's secrets, the light of the world, the salt of the earth, at whose hands all others should take comfort in working, knowledge of God's will, and sight to become children of light, and taste of seasonable wisdom.

They have or should have the Holy Spirit abundantly to pronounce and set forth the word of God, in verity and truth. If ignorance and blindness reign among us, they should with the truth of God's word, instruct and set us in the truth and direct us in the way of the Lord. But thanks be given unto the Lord that hath now sent us such a godly and learned king, in these latter days, to reign over us that, with the virtue and force of God's word, hath taken away the veils and mists of errors, and brought us to the knowledge of the truth, by the light of God's word, which was so long hid and kept under, that the people were nigh famished, and hungered for lack of spiritual food: such was the charity of the spiritual curates and shepherds. But our Moses, and most godly, wise governor and king, hath delivered us out of the captivity and bondage of Pharaoh. I mean by this Moses, king Henry the eighth, my most sovereign favourable lord and husband, one (if Moses had figured any more than Christ), through the excellent grace of God, meet to be another expressed verity of Moses' conquest over Pharaoh. And I mean by this Pharaoh the bishop of Rome, who hath been and is a greater persecutor of all true Christians, than ever was Pharaoh of the children of Israel. For he is a persecutor of the gospel and grace, a setter forth of all superstition and counterfeit holiness, bringing many souls to hell with his alchemy and counterfeit money, deceiving the poor souls under the pretence of holiness: but so much the greater shall be his damnation, because he deceiveth and robbeth under Christ's mantle. The Lord keep and defend all men from his jugglings and sleights, but especially the poor, simple, unlearned souls. And this lesson I would all men had of him, that when they began to mislike his doing, then only begin they to like God, and certainly not before.

As for the spiritual pastors and shepherds, I think they will cleave and stick fast to the word of God, even to the death, to vanquish all God's enemies, if need shall require all respects of honour, dignity, riches, wealth, and their private commodities, laid apart, following also the examples of Christ, and his chosen apostles, in preaching and teaching sincere and wholesome doctrine, and such things as make for peace, with godly lessons, wherewith they may edify others, that every man may walk after his vocation in holiness of life, in unity and concord, which unity is to be desired of all true Christians.

It is much to be lamented, the schisms, varieties, contentions, and disputations that have been and are in the world about Christian religion, and no agreement nor concord of the same among the learned men. Truly the devil hath been the sower of the seed of sedition, and shall be the maintainer of it, even till God's will be fulfilled. There is no war so cruel and evil as this, for the war with sword killeth but the bodies, and this slayeth many souls, for the poor unlearned persons remain confused, and almost every one believeth and worketh after his own way. And yet there is but one truth of God's word, by the which we shall be saved. Happy are they that receive it, and most unhappy are they which neglect and persecute the same. For it shall be more easy for Sodom and Gomorrah, at the day of judgment, than for them [Matt. 11:24]. And not without just cause, if we consider the benevolence, goodness, and mercy of God, who hath declared his charity towards us, greater, and more inestimable, than ever he did to the Hebrews, for they lived under shadows and figures, and were bound to the law [Heb. 10:1]. And Christ (we being his greatest enemies) hath delivered us from the bondage of the law, and hath fulfilled all that was figured in their law, and also in their prophecies, shedding his own precious blood to make us the children of his Father, and his brethren, and hath made us free, setting us in a godly liberty: I mean not licence to sin, as many are glad to interpret the same, when Christian liberty is godly entreated of.

Truly it is no good spirit that moveth men to find fault at every thing, and when things may be well taken, to pervert them into an evil sense and meaning. There are in the world many speakers of holiness and good works, but very rare and seldom is declared which are the good and holy works. The works of the Spirit are almost never spoken of, and therefore very few know what they be. I am able to justify the ignorance of the people to be great, not in this matter alone, but in many others, the which were most necessary for Christians to know. Because I have had just proof of the same, it makes me thus much to say, with no little sorrow and grief in my heart, for such a miserable ignorance and blindness amongst the people.

I doubt not but we can all say, "Lord, Lord," but I fear God may say unto us [Matt. 7:21], "This people honoureth me with their lips, but their hearts are far from me" [Matt. 15:8]. God desireth nothing but the heart, and saith he will be worshiped in spirit and truth [John 4:24]. Christ condemned all hypocrisy and feigned holiness, and taught sincere, pure, and true godliness: but we, worse than frantic, or blind, will not follow Christ's doctrine, but trust to men's doctrines, judgments, and sayings, which dimmeth our eyes, and so the blind lead the blind, and both fall into the ditch. Truly in my simple and unlearned judgment, no man's doctrine is to be esteemed or preferred like unto Christ's and the apostles', nor to be taught as a perfect and true doctrine but even as it doth accord and agree with the doctrine of the gospel.

But yet those that are called spiritual pastors, although they are most carnal, as it doth very evidently and plainly appear by their fruits, are so blinded with the love of themselves, and the world, that they extol men's inventions and doctrines before the doctrine of the gospel. And when they are not able to maintain their own inventions and doctrine with any jot of the scripture, then they most cruelly persecute them that are contrary to the same. Are such the lovers of Christ? Nay, nay they are the lovers of the wicked mammon, neither regarding God nor his honour. For filthy lucre hath made them almost mad, but frantic they are doubtless. Is not this miserable state of spiritual men in the world much to be lamented of all good Christians? But yet I cannot allow, neither praise all kind of lamentation, but such as may stand with Christian charity.

Chapter Eight

The fruits and rules of true Christianity

Charity suffereth long, and is gentle, envieth not, upbraideth no man, casteth frowardly no faults in men's teeth, but referreth all things to God [1 Cor. 13], being angry without sin [Eph. 4:26], reforming others without their slanders, carrying ever a storehouse of mild words to pierce the stony-hearted men. I would that all Christians, like as they have professed Christ, would so endeavour themselves to follow him in godly living. For we have not put on Christ to live any more to ourselves in the vanities, delights, and pleasures of the world, and the flesh, suffering the concupiscence and carnality of the flesh to have its full swing: for we must walk after the Spirit, and not after the flesh, for the spirit is spiritual, and coveteth spiritual things, and the flesh carnal [Gal. 5:16ff], and desireth carnal things. The men, regenerate by Christ, despise the world and all the vanities and pleasures thereof.

They are no lovers of themselves, for they feel how evil and infirm they be, not being able to do any good thing without the help of God, from whom they acknowledge all goodness to proceed. They flatter not themselves with thinking every thing which shineth to the world to be good and holy, for they know all external and outward works, be they ever so glorious and fair to the world, may be done of the evil as well as of the good. And therefore they have in very little estimation the outward show of holiness, because they are all spiritual, casting up their eyes upon heavenly things: neither looking nor regarding the earthly things, for they are to them vile and abject. They have also the simplicity of the dove, and the policy of the serpent [Matt. 10:16]: for by simplicity, they have a desire to do good to all men, and to hurt no man, no though they have occasion given, and by policy, they give not, nor minister any just cause to any man, whereby their doctrine might be reproved. They be not also as a reed shaken with every wind [Matt. 11:7], but when they are blasted with the tempests and storms of the world, then remain they most firm, stable, and quiet, feeling in spirit that God (as their best Father) doth send, and suffer all things for their benefit and commodity. Christ is to them a rule, a line, an example of Christian life. They are never offended at any thing, although occasion be ministered unto them. For like as Christ, when Peter would have withdrawn him from death, answered, and said, "Go back from me Satan, for thou offendest me" [Matt. 16:23], that is, as much as lieth in thee, thou givest me occasion with thy words to make me withdraw myself from death, although I yield not thereto, for this thy procurement cannot extinguish the burning desire I have to shed my blood for my chosen. Even so the perfect men are never offended at anything, for although the world were full of sin, they would not withdraw themselves from doing of good, nor wax cold in the love of the Lord. And much less would they be moved to be evil, yea rather they are so much the more moved to do good.

The regenerated by Christ are never offended at the works of God, because they know by faith that God doth all things well, and that he cannot err, neither for want of power, nor by ignorance nor malice: for they know him to be almighty, and that he seeth all things and is most abundantly good. They see and feel in spirit that of that will most highly perfect cannot but proceed most perfect works. Likewise they are not offended at the works of men. For if they are good, they are moved by them to take occasion to follow them, and to acknowledge the goodness of God, with giving of thanks, and praising his name daily the more. But if they are indifferent, and such as may be done with good and evil intents, they judge the best part, thinking they may be done to a good purpose, and so they are edified. But if they are so evil, that they cannot be taken in good part by any means, yet they are not offended, although occasion be given, nay rather, they are edified, inasmuch as they take occasion to be better, although the contrary be ministered unto them.

Then begin they to think and say thus: "If God had not preserved me with his grace, I should have committed this sin and worse. O how much am I bound to confess and acknowledge the goodness of God." They go also thinking and saying further: "He that hath sinned, may be one of God's elect, peradventure the Lord hath suffered him to fall, to the intent he may the better know himself. I know he is one of them that Christ hath shed his blood for and one of my Christian brethren. Truly I will admonish and rebuke him and in case I find him desperate I will comfort him, and show him the great goodness and mercy of God in Christ: and with godly consolations I will see if I can lift him up." And thus ye may see how the men, regenerated by Christ, of everything, win and receive fruit.

Chapter Nine

Of the fruits of infidelity, and the offence of the weak

And contrary the younglings and imperfect are offended at small trifles, taking every thing in evil part, grudging and murmuring against their neighbor: and so much the more, as they show themselves fervent in their so doing, they are judged of the blind world, and of themselves, great zeal-bearers to God. If this were the greatest evil of these young-lings, it were not the most evil: but I fear they are so blind and ignorant, that they are offended also at good things, and judge nothing good but such as they embrace and esteem to be good, with murmuring against all such as follow not their ways. If there are any of this sort, the Lord give them the light of his truth, that they may increase and grow in godly strength. I suppose if such younglings and imperfect had seen Christ and his disciples eat meat with unwashed hands [Mark 7] or not to have fasted with the Pharisees, they would have been offended, seeing him a breaker of men's traditions. Their affections dispose their eyes to see through other men, and they see nothing in themselves, where charity (although it be most full of eyes to see the faults of others whom it coveteth to amend) thinketh none evil, but discreetly and rightly interpreteth all things, by which more justly and truly everything is taken.

Now these superstitious weaklings, if they had been conversant with Christ, and seen him lead his life, sometime with women, sometime with Samaritans, with Publicans, sinners, and with the Pharisees, they would have murmured at him. Also if they had seen Mary pour upon Christ the precious ointment, they would have said with Judas, "this ointment might have been sold, and given to the poor" [Matt. 26:9]. If they also had seen Christ, with whips, drive out of the temple those that bought and sold [Matt. 21:12], they would forthwith have judged Christ to have been troubled and moved with anger, and not by zeal of charity. How would they have been offended, if they had seen him go to the Jews' feast, heal a sick man upon the sabbath day [John 5], practice with the woman of Samaria [John 4], yea and show unto her of his most divine doctrine and life? They would have taken occasion to have hated and persecuted him, as the scribes and Pharisees did. And even so should Christ, the Saviour of the world, have been to them an offence and ruin.

There are another kind of little ones imperfect, which are offended after this sort and manner: as when they see one that is reputed and esteemed holy, to commit sin, forthwith they learn to do that, and worse, and wax cold in doing of good, and confirm themselves in evil, and then they excuse their wicked life, publishing the same with the slander of their neighbor. If any man reprove them, they say, "such a man did this, and worse." So it is evident that such persons would deny Christ, if they saw other men do the same. If they went to Rome and saw the enormities of the prelates, which are said to reign there among them, I doubt not, if they saw one of them sin, who was reputed and taken for holy, their faith should be lost, but not the faith of Christ, which they never possessed, but they should lose that human opinion which they had of the goodness of the prelates. For if they had the faith of Christ, the Holy Ghost should be a witness unto them, the which should be mighty in them, that, in case all the world would deny Christ, yet they would remain firm and stable in the true faith.

The Pharisees also took occasion of the evil of others, to wax haughty and proud, taking themselves to be men of greater perfection than any others because of their virtue, even as the Pharisee did when he saw the Publican's submission [Luke 18:9–14]. And so they are offended with every little thing, judging evil, murmuring against their neighbor, and for the same, they are of many reputed and taken for the more holy and good, whereas indeed they are the more wicked. The most wicked persons are offended even at themselves, for at their little stability in goodness, and of their detestable and evil life, they take occasion to despair, where they ought the more to commit themselves to God, asking mercy for their offences, and forthwith to give thanks that it hath pleased him of his goodness to suffer them so long a time.

But what needs it any more to say: the evil men are offended even at the works of God. They see God suffer sinners, therefore, think they, sin displeases him not. And because they see not the good rewarded with riches, oftentimes they imagine that God loveth them not. It seemeth to them God is partial, because he hath elected some, and some reproved. And therefore they say, that the elected are sure of salvation, taking by that occasion to do evil enough, saying, "Whatsoever God hath determined, shall be performed." If also they see the good men oppressed and the evil men exalted, they judge God unjust, taking occasion to live evilly, saying, "inasmuch as God favoureth the naughty men, let us do evil enough, to the intent he do us good." If then the wicked be offended even at God, it is no wonder if they are offended at those that follow and walk in his paths and ways.

Chapter Ten

How carnal persons slander the truth of God

Now I will speak with great dolour[8] and heaviness in my heart, of a sort of people which are in the world that are called professors of the gospel, and by their words do declare and show they are much affected to the same. But I am afraid some of them do build upon the sand, as Simon Magus did, making a weak foundation [Acts 12:8–9]. I mean they make not Christ their chiefest foundation, professing his doctrine of a sincere, pure, and zealous mind, but either because they would be called gospellers, to procure some credit and good opinions of the true and very favourers of Christ's doctrine, or to find out some carnal liberty, or to be contentious disputers, finders, or rebukers of other men's faults, or else finally to please and flatter the world: such gospellers are an offence, and a slander to the word of God, and make the wicked to rejoice and laugh at them, saying, "Behold, I pray you, their fair fruits."

What charity? What discretion? What godliness, holiness, or purity of life is among them? Are not they great avengers, foul gluttons, slanderers, backbiters, adulterers, fornicators, swearers, and blasphemers? Yea and wallow and tumble in all sins: these are the fruits of their doctrine. And thus it may be seen how the word of God is evil spoken of through licentious and evil living, and yet the word of God is all

8. *Dolour*: lamentation.

holy, pure, sincere, and godly, being the doctrine and occasion of all holy and pure living. It is the wicked that pervert all good things into evil, for an evil tree cannot bring forth good fruit [Matt. 7:15–20], and when good seed is sown in a barren and evil ground, it yieldeth no good corn, and so it fareth by the word of God [Matt. 13:18–23]. For when it is heard and known of wicked men, it bringeth no good fruit, but when it is sown in good ground, I mean the hearts of good people, it bringeth forth good fruit abundantly, so that the want and fault is in men, and not in the word of God. I pray God all men and women may have grace to become meet tillage for the fruits of the gospel, and to leave only the jangling of it. For only speaking of the gospel makes not men good Christians, but good talkers, except their facts and works agree with the same: so then their speech is good, because their hearts are good. And even as much talk of the word of God, without practicing the same in our living, is evil and detestable in the sight of God, so it is a lamentable thing to hear how there are many in the world that do not well digest the reading of scripture, and do commend and praise ignorance, and say that much knowledge of God's word is the original of all dissension, schisms, and contention, and makes men haughty, proud, and presumptuous by reading of the same.

This manner of saying is no less than a plain blasphemy against the Holy Ghost. For the Spirit of God is the author of his word, and so the Holy Ghost is made the author of evil, which is a most great blasphemy and (as the scripture saith) "a sin that shall not be forgiven in this world, neither in the other to come" [Matt. 12:32]. It were all our parts and duties to procure and seek all the ways and means possible, to have more knowledge of God's word set forth abroad in the world, and not allow ignorance, and discommend knowledge of God's word, stopping the mouths of the unlearned with subtle and crafty persuasions of philosophy and sophistry, whereof comes no fruit, but a great perturbation of the mind to the simple and ignorant, not knowing which way to turn them. For how is it not extreme wickedness to charge the holy, sanctified word of God with the offences of man? To allege the scriptures to be perilous learning, because certain readers thereof fall into heresies?

These men might be enforced by this kind of argument, to forsake the use of fire, because fire burneth their neighbor's house, or to abstain from meat or drink, because they see many surfeit. O blind hate! They slander God for man's offence and excuse the man whom they see offend, and blame the scripture, which they cannot improve. Yea, I have heard of some who have very well understood the Latin tongue, that when they have heard learned men persuade to the credit and belief of certain unwritten verities (as they call them) which are not in scripture expressed, and yet taught as doctrine apostolic, and necessary to be believed, they have been of this opinion, that the learned men have more epistles written by the apostles of Christ, than we have abroad in the canon of the Old and New Testaments, or known of any but only to them of the clergy. Which belief I did not a little lament in my heart to hear, that any creature should have such a blind, ignorant opinion.

Some kind of simplicity is to be praised, but this simplicity, without the verity, I can neither praise nor allow. And thus it may be seen how we, that are unlettered, remain confused, without God of his grace enlighten our hearts and minds with a heavenly light and knowledge of his will, for we are given of ourselves to believe men better than God. I pray God to send all learned men the Spirit of God abundantly, that their doctrine may bring forth the fruits thereof. I suppose there was never more need of good doctrine to be set forth in the world than now in this age: for the carnal children of Adam be so wise in their generation, that if it were possible they would deceive the children of light. The world loveth his own, and therefore their facts and doings are highly esteemed of the world. But the children of God are hated because they are not of the world, for their habitation is in heaven, and they do despise the world as a most vile slave.

The fleshly children of Adam are so politic, subtle, crafty, and wise, in their kind, that the elect should be illuded, if it were possible. For they are clothed with Christ's garment in outer appearance, with a fair show of all godliness and holiness in their words, but they have so shorn, nopped,[9] and turned Christ's garment, and have so disguised themselves, that the children of light, beholding them with a spiritual eye, do account and take them for men which have sold their master's garment, and have stolen a piece of every man's garment. Yet by their subtle art and crafty wits, they have so set those patches and pieces together, that they do make the blind world and carnal men to believe it is Christ's very mantle.

Chapter Eleven

The virtuous children of God

But the children of light know the contrary, for they are led by the Spirit of God to the knowledge of the truth, and therefore they discern and judge all things right, and know from whence they come, even from the bishop of Rome and his members, the headspring of all pride, vainglory, ambition, hypocrisy, and feigned holiness.

The children of God are not abashed, although the world hate them; they believe they are in the grace and favour of

9. *Nopped*: Checked fabric for impurities.

God, and that he as a best Father, doth govern them in all things, putting away from them all vain confidence and trust in their own doings: for they know they can do nothing but sin of themselves. They are not so foolish and childish, not to give God thanks for their election, which was before the beginning of the world. For they believe most surely they are of the chosen, for the Holy Ghost doth witness to their spirit that they are the children of God [Rom. 8:16], and therefore they believe God better than man. They say with St. Paul, "Who shall separate us from the love of God? Shall tribulation, anguish, persecution, hunger, nakedness, peril, or sword? As it is written, For thy sake are we killed all day long, and are counted as sheep appointed to be slain. Nevertheless, in all these things we overcome, through him that loveth us. For I am sure that neither death, nor life, neither angels, nor rule, neither power, neither things present, neither things to come, neither quantity or quality, neither any creature, shall be able to depart us from the love of God, which is in Christ Jesus our Lord" [Rom. 8:31–39].

They are not, by this godly faith, presumptuously inflamed, nor by the same become they loose, idle, or slow in doing of godly works, as carnal men dream of them, so much the more fervent they are in doing most holy and pure works, which God hath commanded them to walk in. They wander not in men's traditions and inventions, leaving the most holy and pure precepts of God undone, which they know they are bound to observe and keep. Also they work not like hirelings, for need, wages, or reward, but as loving children, without respect of lucre, gain, or hire. They are in such liberty of spirit, and joy so much in God, that their inward consolation cannot be expressed with tongue. All fear of damnation is gone from them, for they have put their whole hope of salvation in his hands who will and can perform it. Neither have they any post or pillar to lean to, but

God, and his smooth and unwrinkled church. For he is to them all in all things, and to him they lean, as a most sure square pillar, in prosperity and adversity, nothing doubting of his promises and covenants, for they believe most surely they shall be fulfilled.

Also the children of God are not curious in searching the high mysteries of God, which are not meet for them to know: neither do go about with human and carnal reasons to interpret scripture, persuading men, by their subtle wits and carnal doctrine, that much knowledge of Scripture maketh men heretics, without they temper it with human doctrine, sophistry, philosophy, and logic, wherewith to be seduced according to the traditions of men, after the ordinances of the world, and not after Christ. St. Paul doth most diligently admonish us [Col. 2:8] which arts are not convenient and meet to be made checkmate with scripture: for the scriptures are so pure and holy, that no perfection can be added unto them. For even as fine gold doth excel all other metals, so doth the word of God all men's doctrines. I beseech the Lord to send the learned and unlearned such abundance of his Holy Spirit, that they may obey and observe the most sincere and holy word of God, and show the fruits thereof, which consist chiefly in charity and godly unity: that as we have professed one God, one faith, and one baptism, so we may be all of one mind and one accord, putting away all biting and gnawing: for in backbiting, slandering, and misreporting our Christian brethren, we show not ourselves the disciples of Christ, whom we profess. In him was most high charity, humility, and patience, suffering most patiently all ignominy, rebukes, and slanders, praying to his eternal Father for his enemies with most fervent charity: and in all things did remit his will to his Father's, as the scripture doth witness when he prayed in the mount. A goodly example and lesson for us to follow at all times and seasons, as well in prosperity as in adversity, to have no will but God's will, committing and leaving to him all our cares and griefs, and to abandon all our policies and inventions, for they are most vain and foolish, and indeed very shadows and dreams. But we are yet so carnal and fleshly, that we run headlong, like unbridled colts without snaffle or bit.

If we had the love of God printed in our hearts, it would keep us back from running astray. And until such time as it please God to send us this bit to hold us in, we shall never run the right way, although we speak and talk ever so much of God and his word. The true followers of Christ's doctrine have always a respect and an eye to their vocation. If they are called to the ministry of God's word, they preach and teach it sincerely, to the edifying of others, and show themselves in their living followers of the same. If they are married men, having children and family, they nourish and bring them up, without all bitterness and fierceness, in the doctrine of the Lord, in all godliness and virtue, committing the instruction of others, which appertain not to their charge, to the reformation of God and his ministers, which chiefly are kings and princes, bearing the sword even for that purpose, to punish evil doers [Rom. 13:3]. If they are children, they honour their father and mother [Eph. 6:1], knowing it to be God's commandment, and that he hath thereto annexed a promise of long life. If they are servants, they obey and serve their masters with all fear and reverence [Eph. 6:5], even for the Lord's sake, neither with murmuring nor grudging, but with a free heart and mind.

If they are husbands, they love their wives as their own bodies, after the example as Christ loved the congregation [Eph. 5:28], and gave himself for it, to make it to him a spouse without spot or wrinkle [Eph. 5:26–27]. If they are women married, they learn of St. Paul to be obedient to their husbands, and to keep silence in the congregation, and to learn of their husbands at home [1 Cor. 14:34]. Also they wear such apparel as becometh holiness and comely usage with soberness, not being accusers or detractors, not given to much eating of delicate meats, and drinking of wine, but they teach honest things, to make the young women sober-minded, to love their husbands, to love their children, to be discreet, chaste, housewifely, good, obedient unto their husbands, that the word of God be not evil spoken of [1 Peter 3:1–7]. Verily if all sorts of people would look to their own vocation, and ordain the same, according to Christ's doctrine, we should not have so many eyes and ears to other men's faults as we have. For we are so busy and glad to find and espy out other men's doings that we forget, and can have no time to weigh and ponder our own, which after the word of God, we ought first to reform, and then we shall the better help another with the straw out of his eyes.

But alas we are so much given to love and to flatter ourselves, and so blinded with carnal affections, that we can see and perceive no fault in ourselves. And therefore it is a thing very requisite and necessary for us to pray all, with one heart and mind to God, to give us a heavenly light and knowledge of our own miseries and calamities that we may see them and acknowledge them truly before him.

Chapter Twelve

The conclusion: On living changed lives

If any man shall be offended at this my lamenting the faults of men, which are in the world, fantasizing with themselves that I do it either of hatred or of malice to any sort or kind of people, verily in so doing, they shall do me great wrong. For I thank God, by his grace, I hate no creature: yea, I would say more, to give witness of my conscience, that neither life, honour, riches, neither whatsoever I possess here, which appertaineth to mine own private commodity, be it ever so dearly beloved of me, but most willingly and gladly I would leave it to win any man to Christ, of what degree or sort soever he were. And yet is this nothing in comparison to the charity that God hath showed me, in sending Christ to die for me. No, if I had all the charity of angels and apostles, it should be but like a spark of fire, compared to a great heap of burning coals.

God knoweth of what intent and mind I have lamented mine own sins and faults to the world. I trust nobody will judge that I have done it for praise or thanks of any creature, since rather I might be ashamed than rejoice in rehearsal thereof. For if they knew how little I esteem and weigh the praise of the world, that opinion were soon removed and taken away. For I thank God (by his grace) I know the world to be a blind judge, and the praises thereof vain and of little moment: and therefore I seek not the praises of the same, nor to satisfy it, none otherwise than I am taught by Christ to do, according to Christian charity. I would to God we would all (when occasion doth serve) confess our faults to the world, all respects to our own commodity laid apart. But alas, self love doth so much reign among us, that as I have said before, we cannot espy our own faults. And although sometimes we find our own guilt, either we be favourable to interpret it no sin or else we are ashamed to confess ourselves thereof. Yea and we be sore offended and grieved to hear our faults charitably and godly told us of others, putting no difference between charitable warning and malicious accusing.

Truly if we sought God's glory as we should do in all things, we should not be ashamed to confess ourselves to digress from God's precepts and ordinances, when it is manifest we have done, and daily do. I pray God our own faults and deeds condemn us not at the last day, when every man shall be rewarded according to his doings. Truly if we do not redress and amend our living according to the doctrine of the gospel, we shall receive a terrible sentence of Christ the Son of God, when he shall come to judge and condemn all transgressors and breakers of his precepts and commandments, and to reward all his obedient and loving children. We shall have no man of law to make our plea for us, neither can we have the day deferred, neither will the just Judge be corrupted with affection, bribes, or reward, neither will he hear any excuse or delay, neither shall this saint or that martyr help us, be they ever so holy, neither shall our ignorance save us from damnation. But yet willful blindness, and obstinate ignorance, shall receive greater punishment, and not without just cause. Then shall it be known who hath walked in the dark, for all things shall appear manifest before him. No man's deeds shall be hidden, no neither words nor thoughts. The poor and simple observers of God's commandments shall be rewarded with everlasting life, as obedient children to the heavenly Father. And the transgressors, adders, and diminishers of the law of God, shall receive eternal damnation for their just reward.

I beseech God we may escape this fearful sentence, and be found such faithful servants, and loving children, that we may hear the happy, comfortable, and most joyful sentence ordained for the children of God, which is: "Come hither, ye blessed of my Father, and receive the kingdom of heaven prepared for you before the beginning of the world."

Unto the Father, the Son, and the Holy Ghost be all honour and glory, world without end. Amen.

Finis.

4

THE PERSONAL QUEEN:
SELECTED LETTERS

C oncluding this volume are selected letters to and from Katherine Parr, as well as a few miscellaneous letters of which she is the subject. Beginning with several early letters of Maude Parr regarding her marriage negotiations on Katherine's behalf, and ending with congratulatory letters on the birth of Katherine's daughter, each letter touches on significant persons and events in her life. There are approximately twenty-five surviving letters of Katherine herself, and many others written to her, not all of which appear in this volume. It is probable that many other letters would be available if not for a fire at Wilton, the home of Katherine's brother, William.[1] Introductions are included when necessary. Some of the dates are unknown, and therefore the order is uncertain at times. The letters selected offer the reader a general sense of Katherine's life and character.

1. Agnes Strickland, *Lives of the Queens of England from the Norman Conquests with Anecdotes of Their Courts*, vol. 4 (Philadelphia: Lea and Blanchard, 1848), 89.

Lady Maude Parr to Lord Dacre[2]

July 13, 1524

Maude Parr seeks to arrange a marriage between Katherine and Lord Scrope's son, Henry. Lord Dacre, Lord Scrope's father-in-law and cousin to Katherine's father, Sir Thomas Parr, is enlisted to help make the arrangements.

Most honourable and my very good lord,

I heartily commend me to you. Whereas it pleased you at your last being here to take pains in the matter in consideration of marriage between the lord Scroop's [Scrope's] son and my daughter Katherine, for the which I heartily thank you, at which time I thought the matter in good furtherance. Howbeit, I perceive that my lord Scroop is not agreeable to that consideration. The jointure is little for 1100 marks, which I will not pass, and my said lord will not repay after marriage had; and 200 marks must needs be repaid if my daughter Katherine dies before the age of sixteen, or else I should break Master Parr's will, which I should be loath to do, and there can be no marriage until my lord's son comes to the age of thirteen, and my daughter to the age of twelve, before which time, if the marriage should take none effect, or be dissolved either by death, wardship, disagreement, or otherwise, which may be before that time notwithstanding marriage solemnised, repayment must needs be had of the whole, or else I might fortune to pay my money for nothing. The conversation I had with you at Greenwich, was that I was to pay at desire 1100 marks, 100 on hand—and 100 every year, which is as much as I can

2. Source: Ibid., 13–14.

spare, as you know, and for that my daughter Katherine is to have 100 marks jointure, whereof I am to have 50 marks for her finding til they live together, and then they are to have the whole 100 marks, and repayment to be had if the marriage took not effect. My lord, it might please you to take so much pain as to help conclude this matter, if it will be, and if you see any defect on my part, it shall be ordered as ye deem good, as knoweth Jesus, who preserve your good lordship.

Written at the Rye, the 13th day of July.

Your cousin, Maude Parr.

Lord Dacre to Lord Scrope[3]

December 17, 1524

Lord Dacre encourages Lord Scrope to accept Lady Parr's small dowry. This letter indicates that the Parr household was known for its strong emphasis on education.

My lord,

Your son and heir is the greatest jewel that ye can have, seeing he must represent your own person after your death, unto whom I pray God grant many long years. And if ye be disposed to marry him, I cannot see, without you marry him to an heir of land (which would be right costly), that ye can marry him to so good a stock as my lady Parr, for divers considerations—first, in remembering the wisdom of my said lady, and the good, wise stock of the Greens, whereof she is coming, and also of the wise stock of the

3. Source: Ibid., 14.

Parrs of Kendale, for all wise men do look, when they do marry their child, to the wisdom of the blood they do marry with. I speak not of the possibility of the lady Parr's daughter Katherine, who has but one child between her and 800 marks yearly to inherit thereof.

My lord, the demands you have and my lady's demands are so far asunder, that it is impossible ye can ever agree. I think it is not convenient nor profitable that so large a sum as 100 marks should go yearly out of your land to so young a person as my lady's eldest daughter Katherine, if it fortune, as God defend, that your said son and mine die. Also, I think it good (but I would not have it comprised in the covenant) that, during the time of three years, that he should be with my said lady Parr, if she keep her widowhood, and ye to find him clothing and a servant to wait upon him, and she to find him meat and drink; for I assure you he might learn with her as well as in any place—that I know, as well nurture, as French, and other languages, which me seems were a commodious thing for him.

At Morpeth, 17 day of December, 15 year Henry 8th.

Lord Dacre to Lady Maude Parr[4]

May 25, 1525

Lord Scrope, unimpressed by Maude Parr's offer, refuses to agree to her terms, forcing Lady Parr to end the venture.

Madam,

For my part, I am sorry that ye be thus converted in this matter, seeing the labour I have had in it, which was most for

4. Source: Ibid.,15.

the strength of my friendship for my cousin Katherine, your daughter, assuring you that ye shall not marry Katherine in any place that be so good and comfortable to my said cousin, your daughter. And concerning my lord Scroop's demands, he demandit nothing but that ye were content to give, which was 1100 marks. And concerning his offer, which was 100 marks jointure, it is not far from the custom of the country; for, from the highest to the lowest, it is the custom to give for every 100 marks of dower ten marks jointure.

But finally, madame, seeing ye are thus minded (whereat I am sorry, as nature constraineth me to be), as it doth please you in this business, so it shall please me. And thus, heartily, fare ye well.

At Morpeth, 25th day of May, 16 anno.

Queen Katherine Parr to the Dean and Fellows of Stoke

March 24, 1544

"The Queen recommends Edward Waldegrave, servant to the lord Prince, for a lease in reversion of the manor or farm of Chipley, in Suffolk." [5]

Trusty and well-beloved, we greet you well. And forasmuch as your manor or farm of Chipley in the county of Suffolk lieth in you to let and set at your will and pleasure, and that the same is very commodious for our well-beloved Edward Waldegrave, [6] servant to our most dear and entirely

5. Source: John Bruce, ed., *Correspondence of Matthew Parker, DD: Archbishop of Canterbury, Comprising Letters Written by Him and to Him from A.D. 1535, to His Death, A.D. 1575* (Cambridge: The University Press, 1853), 19–21.

6. Edward was an officer in the household of Princess Mary.

beloved son the lord prince; these therefore shall be heartily to desire and pray you to make a good and sufficient lease in reversion of the same unto the said Edward at this our earnest request: so that he may enjoy the effect of our desire (after the term expired of one Henry Hutton now farmer there) in as large and ample manner as the same Henry now holdeth it, and for so many years as you at the contemplation hereof can find in your heart to bestow on him for our sake. Wherein you shall not only acquire to yourself a farmer well reported of for his honesty and good behaviour, but also minister unto us grateful occasion to have your kind conformity thankfully in our remembrance, whensoever opportunity shall serve us to do you pleasure.

Given under our signet at my lord the King's majesty's palace of Westminster, the 24th of March, the 36th year of his said majesty's most noble and prosperous reign.

Katherine the Queen, K.P.

Queen Katherine Parr to King Henry VIII[7]

July 1544

This letter fragment was written on the occasion of Henry's expedition against France.

Although the distance of time and account of days neither is long nor many of your Majesty's absence, yet the want of your presence, so much desired and beloved by me,

7. Source: John Strype, *Ecclesiastical Memorials Relating Chiefly to Religion and the Reformation of It and the Emergencies of the Church of England under King Henry VIII, King Edward VI, and Queen Mary I with Large Appendixes, Containing Original Papers, Records, &c.*, vol. 2.2 (Oxford: Clarendon Press, 1822), 331–32; see also Strickland, *Lives of the Queens of England*, 39.

maketh me that I cannot quietly pleasure in anything until I hear from your Majesty. The time, therefore, seemeth to me very long, with a great desire to know how your Highness hath done since your departing hence, whose prosperity and health I prefer and desire more than mine own. And whereas I know your Majesty's absence is never without great respects of things, yet love and affection compel me to desire your presence.

And again the same zeal and affection forceth me to be best content with that which is your will and pleasure. Thus love maketh me in all things to set apart mine own commodite and pleasure, and to embrace most joyfully his will and pleasure whom I love. God, the knower of secrets, can judge these words not to be written only with ink, but most truly impressed on the heart. Much more I omit, lest it be thought I go about to praise myself or crave a thank; which thing to do I mind nothing less, but a plain, simple relation of the love and zeal I bear your Majesty, proceeding from the abundance of the heart. Wherein I must confess I desire no worthy commendation, having such just occasion to do the same.

I make like account with your Majesty as I do with God, for his benefits and gifts heaped upon me daily, acknowledging myself a great debtor unto him, not being able to recompense the least of his benefits. In which state I am certain and sure to die; but yet I hope in his gracious acceptation of my good will. Even such confidence have I in your Majesty's gentleness, knowing myself never to have done my duty as were requisite and meet for such a noble Prince, at whose hands I have found and received so much love and goodness, that with words I cannot express it. Lest I should be too tedious to your Majesty, I finish this my scribbled letter, committing you into the governance of the Lord, with long and prosperous life here, and after this life to enjoy the kingdom of his elect.

From Greenwich,

By your Majesty's humble and obedient wife and servant,

Katherine the Queen, K.P.

Queen Katherine Parr to the King's Council[8]

July 25, 1544

Katherine serves as regent of England while the king is at war. Part of his council remains with her; the others accompany the king.[9]

To our right trusty and well-beloved,

We greet you well. Letting you wit that having received your letters of the 23rd of this present, we have by the same had singular comfort, as well to perceive thereby the state of health my lord the king's majesty was in at that present, as also the good beginning of success of his grace's affairs there; for your joyful news whereof we give unto you our right hearty thanks. And forasmuch as, touching the other contents of your said letters, we have presently written at length unto my said lord, the king's majesty, we forbear to repeat the same unto you, not doubting but that his highness will communicate the

8. Source: Mary Anne Everett Wood Green, *Letters of Royal and Illustrious Ladies of Great Britain, from the Commencement of the Twelfth Century to the Close of the Reign of Queen Mary*, vol. 3 (London: Henry Colburn, 1846), 172.

9. Ibid.

same unto you accordingly. Given under our signet at my said lord the king's majesty's honour of Hampton Court, the 25th day of July, the 36th year of his majesty's most noble reign.

Katherine the Queen, K.P.

Queen Katherine Parr to King Henry VIII[10]

July 31, 1544

Here is another letter written during Katherine's regency. The "dowager" is Mary of Guise, the queen consort of James V of Scotland, who serves as regent while their daughter Mary, the future Queen of Scots, is young. Young Mary was promised to Edward VI, but after her mother becomes regent, the agreement is rescinded. Young Mary was sent to France and raised with her new husband-to-be.

To the King's Most Excellent Majesty,

Pleaseth it your majesty to be advertised, this afternoon were brought unto me letters from your majesty's lieutenant of the north, declaring the apprehension of a Scottish ship by certain fishermen of Rye, and in the same certain Frenchmen and Scots, being sent with divers letters and credence towards the French king and others in France. And because I thought this taking of them, with the interception of the said letters, to be of much importance for the advancement of your majesty's affairs, ordained (I doubt not) of God, as well to the intent your highness might thereby certainly understand the crafty dealing and juggling of that nation, as also meet with the same after such sort as

10. Source: Ibid., 173–74.

to your high wisdom shall be thought most convenient; I have presently sent such of the said letters as, upon the view of the same, appeared of most importance unto your majesty. There are a great number of other letters to the French King and others, both from the dowager and others, but they are either of the same effect that these be which I have sent unto your majesty, or general letters only for credence. My lords of your majesty's council have sent to have certain of the chief, both of the Scots and Frenchmen, sent up, upon whose examination your majesty shall be farther advertised with diligence.

My lord prince and the rest of your majesty's children are all, thanks be to God, in very good health. And thus with my most humble commendations unto your majesty, I pray Almighty God have the same in his most blessed keeping. From your majesty's honour of Hampton Court, the last day of July, the 36th year of your majesty's most noble reign.

Your grace's most humble loving wife and servant,

Katherine the Queen, K.P.

Princess Elizabeth to Queen Katherine Parr[11]

July 31, 1544

Inimical fortune, envious of all good and ever revolving human affairs, has deprived me for a whole year of your most illustrious presence, and, not thus content, has yet again robbed me of the same good; which thing would be intolerable to me, did I not hope to enjoy it very soon. And

11. Source: Ibid., 176–77. This letter, originally in Italian, was written during the queen's regency.

in this my exile, I well know that the clemency of your highness has had as much care and solicitude for my health as the king's majesty himself. By which thing I am not only bound to serve you, but also to revere you with filial love, since I understand that your most illustrious highness has not forgotten me every time you have written to the king's majesty, which, indeed, it was my duty to have requested from you. For heretofore I have not dared to write to him. Wherefore I now humbly pray your most excellent highness, that, when you write to his majesty, you will condescend to recommend me to him, praying ever for his sweet benediction, and similarly entreating our Lord God to send him best success, and the obtaining of victory over his enemies, so that your highness and I may, as soon as possible, rejoice together with him on his happy return. No less pray I God, that he would preserve your most illustrious highness; to whose grace, humbly kissing your hands, I offer and recommend myself.

From St. James's, this 31st of July.

Your most obedient daughter, and most faithful servant,

Elizabeth.

Queen Katherine Parr to King Henry VIII[12]

August 25, 1544

To the King's Most Excellent Majesty,

Pleaseth it your majesty to be advertised, albeit I had at this present none occurrents of importance to be signified

12. Source: Ibid., 174.

unto your highness, your realm being, thanks be to Almighty God, in very good order and quiet; yet forasmuch as Richard Higham is at this time dispatched hence unto your majesty with a mass of 30,000*l.*; I thought it my duty to advertise your majesty of the sending of the same; praying Almighty God to send your majesty continuance of health and most prosperous success in all your highness' most noble enterprises. My lord prince and the rest of your majesty's children be in very good health. And thus, with my most humble commendations unto your majesty, I pray Almighty God have the same in his most blessed keeping. From your majesty's honour of Hampton Court, the 25th of August, the 36th year of your majesty's most noble reign.

Your majesty's most humble loving wife and servant,

Katherine the Queen, K.P.

King Henry VIII to Queen Katherine Parr[13]

September 8, 1544

Here is a fragment of a letter from King Henry VIII (in Boulogne, France), reporting on the progress of the campaign against France.

At the closing up of these our letters this day, the castle before named with the dyke is at our command, and not like to be recovered by the Frenchmen again (as we trust), not doubting, with God's grace, but that the castle and town shall shortly follow the same trade, for as this day, which is the eighth of September, we begin three batteries, and have three more going, beside one which hath done

13. Source: Strickland, *Lives of the Queens of England*, 40.

his execution, in shaking and tearing off one of their greatest bulwarks. No more to you at this time, sweetheart, but for lack of time and great occupation of business, saving we pray you to give in our name our hearty blessings to all our children, and recommendations to our cousin Marget,[14] and the rest of the ladies and gentlewomen, and to our council also.

Written with the hand of your loving husband,

Henry R.

Queen Katherine Parr to Princess Mary[15]

September 20, 1544

The translation of Erasmus's Gospel of Saint John into English was dedicated to Queen Katherine. Katherine's desire to publish Erasmus's book in English demonstrates her love for the vernacular, and her employment of Mary to do so points to her regular involvement in the education of the royal children. The fact that this letter was originally written in Latin demonstrates her skill in that language.

Although, most notable and dearest lady, there are many reasons that easily induce my writing to you at this time, yet nothing so greatly moves me thereto as my concern for your health; which, as I hope it is very good, so am I greatly desirous to be assured thereof.

Wherefore, I dispatch to you this messenger, who will be (I judge) most acceptable to you, not only from his skill in

14. Lady Margaret Douglas, Henry's niece (ibid., 40).
15. Source: Green, *Letters of Royal and Illustrious Ladies*, 180–82. Originally in Latin, translation by Green.

music, in which you, I am well aware, take as much delight as myself, but also because, having long sojourned with me, he can give the most certain information of my whole estate and health. And, in truth, I have had it in mind before this to have made a journey to you and salute you in person; but all things do not correspond with my will. Now, however, I hope this winter, and that ere long, that, being nearer, we shall meet; than which, I assure you, nothing can be to me more agreeable, and more to my heart's desire.

Now since, as I have heard, the finishing touch (as far as translation is concerned) is given by Mallet[16] to Erasmus's work upon John, and nought now remains but that proper care and vigilance should be taken in revising, I entreat you to send over to me this very excellent and useful work, now amended by Mallet, or some of your people, that it may be committed to the press in due time; and farther, to signify whether you wish it to go forth to the world (most auspiciously) under your name, or as the production of an unknown writer. To which work you will, in my opinion, do a real injury, if you refuse to let it go down to posterity under the auspices of your own name, since you have undertaken so much labour in accurately translating it for the great good of the public, and would have undertaken still greater (as is well known) if the health of your body had permitted.[17]

And, since all the world knows that you have toiled and laboured much in this business, I do not see why you should repudiate that praise which all men justly confer on you. However, I leave this whole matter to your discretion, and,

16. Francis Mallet, an adviser to Elizabeth when she was queen, was the Master of St. Katherine's Vicar of Stillington, then Canon of Westminster, and later Dean of Lincoln.

17. Desiderius Erasmus, *The First Tome or Volume of the Paraphrase of Erasmus upon the Newe Testamente*, trans. by Nicholas Udall and Mary I, Queen of England (London: Edwarde Whitchurche, 1548).

whatever resolution you may adopt, that will meet my fullest approbation.

For the purse, which you have sent me as a present, I return you great thanks. I pray God, the greatest and best of beings, that He deign to bless you uninterruptedly with true and unalloyed happiness. May you long fare well in him.

From Hanworth, 20th of September.

Most devotedly and lovingly yours,

Katherine the Queen, K.P.

Queen Katherine Parr to Dr. Matthew Parker

November 14, 1544

"Queen Katherine Parr recommends Dr. Parker to appoint Randall Radclyff to the vacant office of bailiff of the college of Stoke."[18]

Trusty and well-beloved doctor Parker, Dean of our college of Stoke, we greet you well. And whereas by credible report we are informed that the bailiwick of our college of Stoke is now void to dispose as you and certain other there shall think it meet and convenient: we therefore heartily desire you, at the contemplation of these our letters, to give the same office unto our well-beloved Randall Radclyff the bearer hereof, who hath already the goodwill of three of those that have interest in the granting of it. So that there rests no farther travail for him, your good will once obtained, the which at this our earnest request, we doubt not but that you will shew and declare effectuously, confirmable to our

18. Source: Bruce, *Correspondence of Matthew Parker*, 16.

desire in this behalf, according to the expectation that we have hitherto conceived in you. Given under signet at my lord the King's majesty's palace of Westminster, the 14th of November, the 36th year of his majesty's most noble reign.

Katherine the Queen, K.P.

Princess Elizabeth to Queen Katherine Parr[19]

December 31, 1544

The Mirror, or Glass, of the Sinful Soul *is a book of French poetry written by Margaret of Navarre (1492–1549), the sister of King Francis I of France, and studied by noble women in France and England. This letter demonstrates Katherine's interest in Elizabeth's education.*

To our most noble and virtuous queen Katherine,

Elizabeth, her humble daughter, wisheth perpetual felicity and everlasting joy.

Not only knowing the effectuous will and fervent zeal, the which your highness hath towards all godly learning, as also my duty towards you, most gracious and sovereign princess; but knowing also, that pusillanimity and idleness are most repugnant unto a reasonable creature, and that (as the philosopher sayeth) even as an instrument of iron or of other metal waxeth soon rusty, unless it be continually occupied; even so shall the wit of a man or a woman wax dull and unapt to do or understand anything perfectly, unless it be always occupied upon some manner of study. Which things considered, hath moved so small a portion as God hath lent me, to prove what I

19. Source: Green, *Letters of Royal and Illustrious Ladies*, 177.

could do. And, therefore, have I (as for essay or beginning, following the right notable saying of the proverb aforesaid) translated this little book out of French rhyme into English prose, joining the sentences together, as well as the capacity of my simple wit and small learning could extend themselves.

The which book is entitled or named, *The Mirror, or Glass, of the Sinful Soul*, wherein is contained, how she (beholding and contemplating what she is), doth perceive how, of herself and her own strength, she can do nothing that good is, or prevaileth for her salvation, unless it be through the grace of God, whose mother, daughter, sister, and wife, by the Scriptures, she proveth herself to be. Trusting also that, through his incomprehensible love, grace, and mercy, she (being called from sin to repentance), doth faithfully hope to be saved. And although I know that, as for my part which I have wrought in it (as well spiritual as manual), there is nothing done as it should be, nor else worthy to come in your grace's hands, but rather all unperfect and uncorrect; yet do I trust also that, howbeit it is like a work which is but new begun and shapen, that the file of your excellent wit and godly learning, in the reading of it (if so it vouchsafe your highness to do), shall rub out, polish, and mend (or else cause to mend), the words (or rather the order of my writing), the which I know, in many places, to be rude, and nothing done as it should be. But I hope that, after to have been in your grace's hands, there shall be nothing in it worthy of reprehension, and that in the mean while no other (but your highness only), shall read it or see it, lest my faults be known of many. Then shall they be better excused (as my confidence is in your grace's accustomed benevolence), than if I should bestow a whole year in writing or inventing ways for to excuse them.

Praying God Almighty, the Maker and Creator of all things, to grant unto your highness the same New Year's day, a lucky and a prosperous year, with prosperous issue, and continuance of many years in good health and continual joy, and all to his honour, praise, and glory.

From Ashridge, the last day of the year of our Lord God, 1544.

Queen Katherine Parr to the University of Cambridge[20]

February 26, 1545

Katherine responds to Cambridge's request that she intercede for it before the king, after an act of Parliament grants him all colleges, chantries, and free chapels.

To our right trusty, dear, and well beloved, the Chancellor and Vice-chancellor of my lord the King's Majesty's University of Cambridge, and to the whole said University there.

Your letters I have received, presented on all your behalfs by Mr Doctor Smith,[21] your discreet and learned advocate. And as they be Latinly written, which is so signified unto me by those that be learned in the Latin tongue, so (I know) you could have uttered your desires and opinions familiarly in your vulgar tongue, aptest for my intelligence: albeit you seem to have conceived rather partially than truly a favourable estimation both of my going forward and dedication to learning, which to advance, or at the least conserve, you by your letters move me diversly, shewing how agreeable it is to me, being in this worldly estate, not only for mine own part to be studious, but also a

---

20. Source: Bruce, *Correspondence of Matthew Parker*, 36; see also Strickland, *The Lives of the Queens of England*, 48; Strype, *Ecclesiastical Memorials*, 2.2:337–38.

21. Sir Thomas Smith, secretary to Edward VI.

maintainer and a cherisher of the learned state, by bearing me in hand that I am endued and perfected with those qualities and respects which ought to be in a person of my vocation.

Truly this your discreet and politic document I as thankfully accept as you desire that I should embrace it. And for as much (as I do hear) all kind of learning doth flourish amongst you in this age, as it did amongst the Greeks at Athens long ago, I desire you all not so to hunger for the exquisite knowledge of profane learning, that it may be thought the Greeks' University was but transposed, or now in England again revived, forgetting our Christianity, since their excellency only did attain to moral and natural things. But rather I gently exhort you to study and apply those doctrines as means and apt degrees to the attaining and setting forth the better Christ's reverent and most sacred doctrine: that it may not be laid against you in evidence, at the tribunal sent of God, how you were ashamed of Christ's doctrine: for this Latin lesson I am taught to say of Saint Paul, *non me pudet evangelii*; to the sincere setting forth whereof (I trust) universally in all your vocations and ministries you will apply and conform your sundry gifts, arts, and studies, to such end and sort, that Cambridge may be accounted rather an University of divine philosophy than of natural or moral, as Athens was. Upon the confidence of which your accomplishment to my expectation, zeal, and request, I (according to your desires) have attempted my lord the King's Majesty, for the establishment of your livelihood and possessions; in which, notwithstanding his Majesty's property and interest, through the consent of the high court of parliament, his highness being such a patron to good learning, doth tender you so much, that he will rather advance learning and erect new occasion thereof, than to confound those your ancient and godly institutions: so that learning may hereafter justly ascribe her very original, whole conservation, and sure stay to our Sovereign Lord, her only defence and worthy ornament: the prosperous estate and princely government of whom long to preserve, I doubt not but every of you will with daily invocation call upon him, who alone and only can dispose all to every creature.

Scribbled with the hand of her that prayeth to the Lord and immortal God, to send you all prosperous success in godly learning and knowledge.

From my Lord the King's Majesty's manor of Greenwich, the 26th of February.

Katherine the Queen, KP.

Prince Edward to Queen Katherine Parr[22]

May 12, 1546

Pardon my rude style in writing to you, most illustrious Queen and beloved mother, and receive my hearty thanks for your loving kindness to me and my sister. Yet, dearest mother, the only true consolation is from Heaven, and the only real love is the love of God. Preserve, therefore, I pray you, my dear sister Mary from all the wiles and enchantments of the evil one, and beseech her to attend no longer to foreign dances and merriments which do not become a most Christian Princess. And so, putting my trust in God for you to take this exhortation in good part, I commend you to his most gracious keeping.

From Hunsdon, this 12th of May.

Edward the Prince.

22. Source: John Gough Nichols, *Literary Remains of King Edward the Sixth, Edited from His Autograph Manuscripts with Historical Notes and a Biographical Memoir*, vol. 1 (New York: Burt Franklin, 1857), 9.

Prince Edward to Queen Katherine Parr[23]

1546

Most honourable and entirely beloved mother, I have me most humbly recommended unto your grace, with like thanks, both for that your grace did accept so gently my simple and rude letters, and also that it pleased your grace so gently to vouchsafe to direct unto me your loving and tender letters, which do give me much comfort and encouragement to go forward in such things wherein your grace beareth me on hand that I am already entered. I pray God I may be able in part to satisfy the good expectation of the king's majesty my father and of your grace: whom God have ever in his most blessed keeping.

Your loving son,

E. Prince.

Prince Edward to Queen Katherine Parr[24]

May 24, 1546

Edward, the Prince, to the most illustrious Queen, his mother,

Perhaps you will be surprised that I so often write to you, and that in so short a time, most noble queen and most

23. Sources: Ibid., 1:13; Strickland, *Lives of the Queens of England*, 50.
24. Source: James Orchard Halliwell, *Letters of the Kings of England, Now First Collected from the Originals in Royal Archives, and from Other Authentic Sources, Private as Well as Public* (London: Henry Colburn, 1846), 9; Nichols, *Literary Remains*, 1:12. Nichols notes that another copy of this letter has the date as May 11.

dear mother; but by the same rule you may be surprised that I do my duty towards you. However, this I am now doing more willingly, because I have got a suitable messenger, my servant; and therefore I could not help sending a letter to you, in order to testify my respect and affection.

Fare thee well, most noble Queen.

At Hunsdon, 24th of May.

Your most obsequious son,

Edward the Prince.

Prince Edward to Queen Katherine Parr[25]

June 10, 1546

*The queen impressed Edward with a previous letter she had written in Italian (*Romanis literis*). As argued in the first chapter of this volume, this letter refers to Katherine's progress in the Latin translation of Erasmus, not to her progress in the Latin tongue.*

Although all your letters are sweet to me, yet these last were pleasing beyond the rest, most noble queen and most kind mother; for which I return you exceeding thanks. But truly by these I perceive that you have given your attention to the Roman characters, so that my preceptor could not be persuaded but that your secretary wrote them, till he observed your name written equally well. I also was much surprised. I hear too, that your highness is progressing in the Latin tongue and in the *bonis literis* [good literature]. Wherefore I feel no little joy, for letters are lasting; but other

25. Source: Halliwell, *Letters of the Kings of England*, 12–13.

things that seem so perish. Literature also conduces to virtuous conduct, but ignorance thereof leads to vice. And, just as the sun is the light of the world, so is learning the light of the mind. Every thing that comes from God, is good; learning comes from God, therefore learning is good.

A certain one[26] hath also said, "what you see, you shall not long see;" signifying, that riches and the other goods of this life will perish.

I pray the power celestial that he keep your highness in safety.

At Hunsdon, 10th of June, 1546.

Queen Katherine Parr to Lady Wriothesley[27]

1546

Katherine comforts Lady Wriothesley, the wife of her enemy, Thomas Wriothesley, after the loss of her only son.

Good my lady Wriothesley, understanding it hath pleased God of late to disinherit your son of this world, of intent he should become partner and chosen heir of the everlasting inheritance, for which calling and happy vocation ye may rejoice, yet when I consider you are a mother by flesh and nature, doubting how you can give place quietly to the same; inasmuch as Christ's mother, endued with all godly virtues, did utter a sorrowful natural passion of her Son's death, whereby we have all obtained everlastingly to live—

26. This "certain one" is Ludovico Vives, and his name appears in this place in the Latin edition from Nichols (Nichols, *Literary Remains*, 1:16).

27. Source: Religious Tract Society, *Writings of Edward the Sixth, William Hugh, Queen Catherine Parr, Anne Askew, Lady Jane Grey, Hamilton, and Balnaves* (London: The Religious Tract Society, 1836), 14. Date is uncertain, but believed to be after the event with Thomas.

therefore amongst other discreet and godly consolations given unto you, as well by my lord your husband, as other your wise friends, I have thought with mine own hand to recommend unto you my simple counsel and advice; desiring you not so to utter your natural affection by inordinate sorrow, that God have cause to take you as a murmurer against his appointments and ordinances. For what is excessive sorrow but a plain evidence against you, that your inward mind doth repine against God's doings, and a declaration that you are not contented, that God hath put your son by nature, but his by adoption, in possession of the heavenly kingdom? Such as have doubted of the everlasting life to come, do sorrow and bewail the departure hence, but those which are persuaded that to die here is life again, do rather hunger for death, and count it a felicity, than to bewail it as an utter destruction.

How much, madam, are you to be counted godly wise, that will and can prevent, through your godly wisdom, knowledge, and humble submission, that thing which time would at length finish. If you lament your son's death, you do him great wrong, and show yourself to sorrow for the happiest thing that ever came to him, being in the hands of his best Father. If you are sorry for your own commodity, you show yourself to live to yourself. And as of his towardness you could but only hope, his years were so young which could perform nothing, it seemeth that he was now a meet and pleasant sacrifice for Christ.

Wherefore, good my lady Wriothesley, put away all immoderate and unjust heaviness, requiring you with thanksgiving to frame your heart, that the Father in heaven may think you are most glad and best contented to make him a present of his spiritual, and your only natural son; glorifying him more in that it hath pleased his majesty to accept and able him to his kingdom, than that it first pleased him to comfort you with such a gift; who can at his pleasure recompense your loss with such a like jewel, if gladly and quietly you submit, and refer all to his pleasure.

Katherine the Queen, K.P.

Prince Edward to Queen Katherine Parr[28]

August 12, 1546

Most noble queen and most illustrious mother, I give you uncommon thanks, that you behaved to me so kindly, when I was with you at Westminster. This gentle behaviour doth put my love to the test, although I cannot love you better. Therefore, to me it seems an age since I saw you. Therefore I would entreat your highness to pardon me, that I have not, this long time, written a letter to you. I did indeed wish it, but daily I have been expecting to be with your highness. But, when Fowler[29] went away, I had scarcely time for writing to the king's majesty.

Further, I entreat your highness to let me know, whether the Lord-High Admiral,[30] who is coming from France, understands Latin well; for, if he does, I should wish to learn further what I may say to him, when I shall come to meet him.

I pray God to guard you, and give you learning and virtue, the safest riches.

12th August, 1546.

28. Source: Halliwell, *Letters of the Kings of England*, 15–16.

29. Halliwell is missing this name, but Nichols has Fowler, Latin *Foulerus* (Nichols, *Literary Remains*, 1:22–23).

30. This would be Claude d'Annebaut, who was to represent France in the signing of a treaty of peace (see Nichols, *Literary Remains*, 1:22).

Prince Edward to Queen Katherine Parr[31]

January 10, 1547

That I have not written to you so long, most illustrious Queen and dearest mother, the reason is, not negligence, but over-earnestness; for I need not this, because I did not purpose to write at all, but to write with more correctness. Wherefore, I hope you will be satisfied and glad that I have not written before; for you wish me to improve all my genteel accomplishment and piety, which is a token of your signal and lasting love towards me. And this love you have manifested to me by many kindnesses, and specially by this New-year's gift, which you have lately sent to me, wherein the king's majesty's image and your own is contained, expressed to the life. For it delighteth me much to gaze upon your likenesses, though absent, whom, with the greatest pleasure, I would see present; and to whom I am bounden, as well by nature as by duty. Wherefore, I give you greater thanks for this New-year's gift than if you had sent me costly garments or embossed gold or any other magnificent thing.

May God keep in safety and health your highness, whom I hope to visit shortly.

At Hatfield, 10th January, 1546.[32]

King Edward VI to Queen Katherine Parr[33]

February 7, 1547

31. Sources: Halliwell, *Letters of the Kings of England*, 22–23; Nichols, *Literary Remains*, 1:33.

32. Because a new year had begun, it is likely that Edward wrote the incorrect year at the bottom of his letter. The date of 1547 is preferred.

33. Source: Halliwell, *Letters of the Kings of England*, 25.

Written from the Tower of London on the occasion of Henry's death.

Many thanks for the letter that you last sent to me, dearest mother; which is a token of your singular and daily love to me. And now, as it hath seemed good to God, the greatest and best of beings, that my father and your husband, our most illustrious sovereign, should end this life, it is a common grief to both. This, however, consoles us, that he is now in heaven, and that he hath gone out of this miserable world into happy and everlasting blessedness. For whoever here leads a virtuous life, and governs the state aright, as my noble father has done, who ever promoted piety and banished all ignorance, hath a most certain journey into heaven. Although nature prompts us to grieve and shed tears for the departure of him now gone from our eyes, yet Scripture and wisdom prompt us to moderate those feelings, lest we appear to have no hope at all of the resurrection of the dead. Besides, as your highness has conferred on me so many benefits, I ought to afford you whatever comfort I can. I wish your highness abundant health. Farewell, revered queen.

From the Tower, 7th of February, 1547.

Edward the King.

King Edward VI to Queen Dowager Katherine Parr[34]

1547

I thank you, very noble and excellent queen, for your letter which you have sent me lately, not only for the beauty of

34. Source: Ibid., 33, originally in French.

the characters, but also for having invented the same characters; for, when I saw your beautiful letter and the excellence of your ingenuity, surpassing greatly my invention, I dared not to write to you. But, when I reflected that your disposition was so good, that everything proceeding from a good spirit and will was acceptable to you, I wrote to you this letter.

From my house at Hampton Court,

Edward.

Princess Elizabeth to Admiral Seymour[35]

February 27, 1547

Historians believe that Lord Seymour had his eyes fixed on the young Elizabeth from the start. Elizabeth's "let's be friends" letter demonstrates that Seymour first approached her after Henry's death, only to be rejected and then move on to Katherine. Katherine may not have been immediately aware, but sometime after her marriage to Seymour his interest became apparent as he consistently attempted to seduce Elizabeth, then under Katherine's care. After several disturbing episodes, Katherine had Elizabeth removed, presumably for her own safety and reputation.

My Lord Admiral,

The letter you have written to me is the most obliging, and at the same time the most eloquent in the world. And as I do not feel myself competent to reply to so many courteous expressions, I shall content myself with unfolding to you, in few words, my real sentiments. I confess to you that your let-

35. Source: Green, *Letters of Royal and Illustrious Ladies*, 191.

ter, all elegant as it is, has very much surprised me; for, besides that neither my age nor my inclination allows me to think of marriage, I never could have believed that anyone would have spoken to me of nuptials, at a time when I ought to think of nothing but sorrow for the death of my father. And to him I owe so much, that I must have two years at least to mourn for his loss. And how can I make up my mind to become a wife before I shall have enjoyed for some years my virgin state, and arrived at years of discretion?

Permit me, then, my lord admiral, to tell you frankly, that, as there is no one in the world who more esteems your merit than myself, or who sees you with more pleasure as a disinterested person, so would I preserve to myself the privilege of recognizing you as such, without entering into that strict bond of matrimony, which often causes one to forget the possession of true merit. Let your highness be well persuaded that, though I decline the happiness of becoming your wife, I shall never cease to interest myself in all that can crown your merit with glory, and shall ever feel the greatest pleasure in being your servant, and good friend,

Elizabeth

Queen Katherine Parr to Thomas Seymour[36]

1547

With the passing of Henry, Katherine and Thomas renew their courtship. A handful of love letters between the two have survived, clearly indicating that, at least for Katherine, previous romantic feelings never fully subsided.

My lord:

36. Source: Strickland, *Lives of the Queens of England*, 67.

4.1 A sample of Katherine Parr's handwriting. This is the 1547 letter to Thomas Seymour in which they renew their courtship. (See below.)

I send you my most humble and hearty commendations, being desirous to know how ye have done since I saw you. I pray you be not offended with me, in that I send sooner to you than I said I would, for my promise was but once in a fortnight. Howbeit, the time is well abbreviated, by what means I know not, except the weeks be shorter at Chelsea than in other places. My lord, your brother, hath deferred answer concerning such requests as I made to him till his coming hither, which he saith shall be immediately after the term. This is not his first promise I have received of his coming, and yet unperformed. I think my lady[37] hath taught him that lesson; for it is her custom to promise many comings to her friends, and to perform none. I trust in greater matters she is more circumspect. And thus, my lord, I make an end, bidding you most heartily farewell, wishing you the good I would myself. From Chelsea.[38]

I would not have you to think that this mine honest goodwill towards you to proceed of any sudden motion of passion; for, as truly as God is God, my mind was fully bent, the other time I was at liberty, to marry you before any man I know. Howbeit, God withstood my will therein most vehemently for a time, and through his grace and goodness made that possible which seemeth to me most impossible; that was, made me to renounce utterly mine own will, and to follow his will most willingly. It were too long to write all the process of this matter. If I live, I shall declare it to you myself. I can say nothing, but as my lady of Suffolk[39] saith, "God is a marvellous man."

By her that is yours to serve and obey during her life,

Katherine the Queen, K.P.

37. Anne Stanhope was the wife of Edward Seymour and Duchess of Somerset.
38. Parr had intended to end the letter with "From Chelsea" but then continued.
39. Katherine Willoughby was the wife of Charles Brandon and Duchess of Suffolk. She was a lady-in-waiting to Katherine Parr and a Protestant.

Queen Katherine Parr to Thomas Seymour[40]

May 1547

My lord,

As I gather by your letter, delivered to my brother Herbert,[41] ye are in some fear how to frame my lord your brother to speak in your favour, the denial of your request shall make his folly more manifest to the world, which will more grieve me than the want of his speaking. I would not wish you to importune for his good-will, if it come not frankly at the first; it shall be sufficient once to require it, and then to cease. I would desire you might obtain the king's letters in your favour, and also the aid and furtherance of the most notable of the council, such as you shall think convenient: which thing obtained shall be no small shame to your brother and loving sister, in case they do not the like.[42]

My lord, whereas ye charge me with a promise, written with mine own hand, to change the two years into two months, I think ye have no such plain sentence written with my hand. I know not whether you be a paraphraser or not. If you be learned in that science, it is possible ye may of one word make a whole sentence, and yet not at all times alter the true meaning of the writer, as it appeareth, by this your exposition upon my writing.

When it shall be your pleasure to repair hither, ye must take some pain to come early in the morning, that ye may be gone again by seven o'clock; and so I suppose, ye may come without suspect. I pray you let me have knowledge

---

40. Source: Strickland, *Lives of the Queens of England*, 68. Katherine and Thomas Seymour, in order to avoid impropriety, were privately married, a fact that was not made public for several months.

41. William Herbert, the husband of Katherine's sister, Anne.

42. Edward and Anne Seymour. The designation "loving" is sarcasm, since Katherine and Anne did not get along.

overnight at what hour ye will come, that your portress may wait at the gate to the fields for you. And thus, with my most humble and hearty commendations, I take my leave of you for this time, giving you like thanks for your coming to Court when I was there.

From Chelsea.

P.S. I will keep in store till I speak with you, my lord's large offer of Fausterne, at which time I shall be glad to know your further pleasure therein.

By her that is, and shall be, your humble, true, and loving wife during her life,

Katherine the Queen, K.P.

Thomas Seymour to Queen Katherine Parr[43]

May 17, 1547

To The Queen's Grace

After my humble commendation unto your highness, yesternight I supped at my brother Herbert's,[44] of whom, for your sake besides mine own, I received good cheer. And after the same, I received from your highness, by my sister Herbert, your commendations, which were more welcome than they were sent. And after the same, she waded further with me touching my lodging with your highness at Chelsea, which I denied lodging with your highness, but that

---

43. Source: Strickland, *Lives of the Queens of England*, 69–70.
44. Strickland notes that since Thomas is calling Herbert his brother, he and Katherine were probably already married (ibid., 69).

indeed I went by the garden as I went to the Bishop of London's house, and at this point stood with her a long time, till at last, she told me further tokens, which made me change my colours, who, like a false wench, took me with the manner. Then, remembering what she was, and knowing how well ye trusted her, examined whether those things came from your highness or were feigned. She answered that they came from your highness and he, that he knew it to be true, for the which I render unto your highness my most humble and hearty thanks. For by her company, in default of yours, I shall shorten the weeks in these parts, which heretofore were four days longer in every one of them than they were under the plummet at Chelsea. Besides this commodity, I may also inform your highness by her, how I do proceed in my matter, although I should lack my old friend, Walter Errol. I have not as yet attempted my strength for that I would be first thoroughly in credit, ere I would move the same, but beseeching your highness that I may not so use my said strength that they shall think and hereafter cast in my teeth that by their suit I sought and obtained your goodwill, for hitherto I am out of all their dangers for any pleasure that they have done for me worthy of thanks, and as I judge, your highness may say the like. Wherefore, by mine advice, we will keep us so, nothing mistrusting the goodness of God, but we shall be able to live out of their danger as they shall out of ours. Yet I mean not but to use their friendship to bring our purpose to pass, as occasion shall serve. If I knew by what mean I might gratify your highness for your goodness to me, showed at our last lodging together, it should not be slack to declare mine to you again, and to that intent that I might be more bound unto your highness, that once in three days I might receive three lines in a letter from you, and as many lines and letters more as shall seem good unto your highness. Also, I shall humbly desire your highness to give me one of your small pictures, if ye have any left, who with his silence, shall give me occasion to think on the friendly cheer that I shall receive when my suit shall be at an end; and thus, for fear of troubling your highness with my long and rude letter, I take my leave of your highness, wishing that my hap may be one so good, that I may declare so much by mouth at the same hour that this was writing, which was twelve of the clock in the night, this Tuesday, the 17th of May, at St. James's.

I wrote your highness a line in my last letter, that my lord of Somerset[45] was going to that shire, who hath been sick, which by the [manner] thereof, and as I understand, may get thither as to-morrow.

From him whom ye have bound to honour, love, and in all lawful things obey,

T. Seymour.

King Edward VI to Queen Katherine Parr[46]

May 30, 1547

As I was so near to you, and saw you, or expected to see you every day, I wrote no letter to you, since letters are tokens of remembrance and kindness between those who are at a great distance. But being urged by your request, I would not abstain longer from writing—first, that I may do what is acceptable to you, and then to answer the letter you wrote to me when you were at St. James's, in which, first,

45. Edward Seymour, Duke of Somerset.
46. Source: Latin available in Nichols, *Literary Remains*, vol. 1, 41–42; translation from Strickland, *Lives of the Queens of England*, 71; also in Strype, *Ecclesiastical Memorials*, 2.1:59–60, and Halliwell, *Letters of the Kings of England*, 33.

you set before my eyes the great love you bear my father the king, of most noble memory, then your good-will towards me, and lastly, your godliness and knowledge, and learning in the Scriptures. Proceed, therefore, in your good course; continue to love my father, and to show the same great kindness to me which I have ever perceived in you. Cease not to love and read the Scriptures, but persevere in always reading them; for in the first you show the duty of a good wife and a good subject, and in the second, the warmth of your friendship, and in the third, your piety to God.

Wherefore, since you love my father, I cannot but much esteem you; since you love me, I cannot but love you in return; and, since you love the Word of God, I do love and admire you with my whole heart. Wherefore, if there be any thing wherein I may do you a kindness, either in word or deed, I will do it willingly.

Farewell, this 30th of May.

E. Rex.

King Edward VI to Queen Dowager Katherine Parr[47]

June 25, 1547

A letter from King Edward (age ten) congratulating Katherine on her marriage to Seymour.

We thank you heartily, not only for the gentle acceptation of our suit moved unto you, but also for the loving accomplishing of the same, wherein you have declared, not only a desire to gratify us, but also moved us to declare the

47. Source: Strickland, *Lives of the Queens of England*, 72; also in Strype, *Ecclesiastical Memorials*, 2.1:208–9; Nichols, *Literary Remains*, vol. 1., 44–47.

good-will, likewise, that we bear to you in all your requests. Wherefore ye shall not need to fear any grief to come or to suspect lack of aid in need, seeing that he, being mine uncle, is of so good a nature that he will not be troublesome by any means unto you, and I of such mind, that for divers just causes I must favour you. But even as without cause you merely require help against him whom you have put in trust with the carriage of these letters, so may I merely return the same request unto you, to provide that he may live with you also without grief, which hath given him wholly unto you. And I will so provide for you both, that if hereafter any grief befall, I shall be a sufficient succour in your godly or praiseable enterprises.

Fare ye well, with much increase of honour and virtue in Christ.

From St. James, the fifth and twenty day of June.

Edward.

Queen Katherine Parr to Thomas Seymour[48]

1548

My lord,

This shall be to advertise you, that my lord, your brother, hath this afternoon a little made me warm. It was fortunate we were so much distant, for I suppose else I should have

48. Sources: Strickland, *Lives of the Queens of England*, 73; Samuel Haynes, AM, *A Collection of State Papers Relating to Affairs in the Reigns of King Henry VIII, King Edward VI, Queen Mary, and Queen Elizabeth, from the Year 1542–1570, Transcribed from Original Letters and Other Authentik Memorials, Never Before Published, Left by William Cecill Lord Burghle*, vol. 1 (London: William Bowyer, 1740), 61.

bitten him. What cause have they to fear having such a wife?[49] To-morrow or else upon Saturday at afternoon about three o'clock I will see the king, where I intend to utter all my choler to my lord, your brother, if you shall not give me advice to the contrary; for I would be loath to do anything to hinder your matter. I will declare unto you how my lord hath used me concerning Fausterne, and after I shall most humbly desire you to direct mine answer to him in that behalf. It liketh him to-day to send my Chancellor[50] to me, willing him to declare to me, that he had bought Master Long's[51] lease, and that he doubted not but I would let him enjoy the same to his commodity, wherein I should do to his succession no small pleasure; nothing considering his honour which this matter toucheth not a little, for so much as I at sundry times declared unto him the only cause of my repair into those parts was for the commodity of that park, which else I would not have done. He, notwithstanding, hath so used the matter with giving Master Long such courage that he refuseth to receive such cattle as are brought for the provision of my house; and so, in the mean time, I am forced to commit them to farmers. My lord, I beseech you, send me word with speed, how I shall use myself to my new brother. And thus I take my leave with my most humble and hearty commendations, wishing you all your godly desires, and so well to do as I would myself and better.

From Chelsea in great haste.

49. At this point in the letter, Susan E. James adds the line "It is requisite for them continually to pray for a short dispatch of that hell" (Kateryn Parr: The Making of a Queen [Aldershot, England: Ashgate, 1999], 409). Line does not appear in my copy, but probably belongs in the original.

50. Thomas Arundell was a gentleman of the privy chamber to Cardinal Wolsey. He was executed for treason in 1552.

51. Henry Longe.

By your humble, true, and loving wife in her heart,

Katherine the Queen, K.P.

Queen Katherine Parr to Thomas Seymour[52]

1548

To My Lord,

This shall be to desire you to receive my humble and most hearty recommendations and thanks for your letter, which was no sooner come than welcome. I perceive ye have had no little trouble and business with your matter. I never thought the contrary, but ye should have much ado to bring it to pass as ye would have it. Nevertheless, I supposed my Lord Protector would have used no delay with his friend and natural brother in a matter which is upright and just, as I take it. What will he do to other[s] that be indifferent to him? I judge not very well. I pray God he may deceive me, for his own wealth and benefit more than for mine own. Now I have uttered my choler I shall desire you, good my lord, with all heart not to unquiet yourself with any of his unfriendly parts, but bear them for the time as well as ye can, which I know is much better than either mine advice or doing can express. I am very sorry for the news of the Frenchmen. I pray God it be not a let to our journey. As soon as ye know what they will do, good my lord, I beseech you let me hear from you, for I shall not be very quiet till I know. I gave your little knave your blessing, who like an honest man stirred apace after and before. For Mary Odell[53] being a Bed with me had laid her hand upon

52. Source: Haynes, *State Papers*, 62.
53. Katherine's midwife.

my belly to feel it stir. It hath stirred these three days every morning and evening so that I trust when ye come it will make you some pastime. And thus I end bidding my sweetheart and loving husband better to fare than myself.

From Hanworth, this Saturday in the morning.

My lord, I thank you with all my heart for Master Hutton,[54] desiring you to continue his good, or else I fear me he shall never live in quiet with my Lord Dacres, to whom I pray you make my recommendations, assuring him that I will be his friend, in case he use Master Hutton well, or else, his enemy.

By your most loving, obedient, and humble wife,

Katherine the Queen, K.P.

Thomas Seymour to Queen Katherine Parr[55]

June 9, 1548

Seymour is away at court, attempting to get his brother, Edward, to restore Katherine's property to her. The property had been given to her by her mother and by the king, and was probably refused to Katherine because of her relationship with Seymour. The tension between the two brothers complicates the dispute.

To The Queen's Highness at Hanworth

54. Cuthbert Hutton.

55. Source: Strickland, *Lives of the Queens of England*, 76; portions in italics are gaps filled in from Patrick Fraser Tytler, *England under the Reigns of Edward VI and Mary with the Contemporary History of Europe Illustrated in a Series of Original Letters Never Before Printed*, vol. 1 (London: Richard Bentley, 1839), 102–4.

After my humble commendations and thanks for your letter. As I was perplexed heretofore with unkindness, that I should not have justice of those that I thought would in all my causes been partial, *which did not a little trouble me*; even so, the receiving of your letter revived my spirits, partly, for that I do perceive you be armed with patience, howsoever the matter *will weigh, as chiefest, that I hear my little man doth shake his poll, trusting if* God should give him life to live as long as his father, he will revenge such wrongs *as neither you nor I can, at this present,* the [turmoil] is such—God amend it![56]

Now to put you in some hope again. This day, a little before the receiving of your letter, I have spoken to my lord,[57] whom I have so well handled that he is somewhat qualified. And, although I am in no hopes thereof, yet I am in no despair. I have also broken with him for your mother's gift, who makes answer, that at the finishing of your matter, either to have your own again, or else some recompense as ye shall be content withal. I spake to him of your going down into the country on Wednesday, who was sorry thereof, trusting that I would be here all to-morrow to hear what the Frenchmen will do.[58] But on Monday dinner, I trust to be with you. As for the Frenchmen, I have no mistrust that they shall be any let of my going with you this journey, or any of my continuance there with your highness: and thus, till that time, I bid your highness most heartily well to fare, and thank you for your news, which were right heartily welcome to me.

56. The little boy that Seymour and Katherine assumed they would have turned out to be a little girl, Mary.

57. Edward Seymour, Duke of Somerset.

58. "The Earl of Warwick wrote to William Cecil on 5 June, four days before Seymour wrote this letter, that the French meant to attack Pevensey Castle in Sussex" (Susan E. James, *Kateryn Parr: The Making of a Queen* [Aldershot, England: Ashgate, 1999], 412).

And so I pray to you to show him, with God's blessing and mine; and of all good wills and friendship, I do desire your highness to keep the little knave so lean and gaunt with your good diet and walking, that he may be so small that he may creep out of a mousehole. And so I bid my most dear and well-beloved wife most heartily well to fare.

From Westminster, this Saturday, the 9th of June.

Your highness's most faithful, loving husband,

T. Seymour.

Princess Elizabeth to Queen Katherine Parr[59]

ca. June 1548

Elizabeth is no longer living with Katherine, as a result of Thomas Seymour's not-so-subtle advances. This was written to Katherine during her troubled pregnancy.

To the Queen's Highness,

Although I could not be plentiful in giving thanks for the manifold kindness received at your Highness' hand at my departure, yet I am something to be borne withall, for truly I was replete with sorrow to depart from your Highness, especially leaving you undoubtful of health: and, albeit I answered little, I weighed it more deeper, when you said you would warn me of all evils that you should

---

59. Source: Tytler, *England under the Reigns of Edward VI and Mary*, 69–70. Many dates have been offered for this letter, but the date above best corresponds to Katherine's illness. For more information see Leah S. Marcus, Janel Mueller, and Mary Beth Rose, *Elizabeth I: Collected Works* (Chicago: University of Chicago Press, 2000), 17.

hear of me; for if your Grace had not a good opinion of me, you would not have offered friendship to me that way, that all men judge the contrary. But what may I more say, than thank God for providing such friends to me; desiring God to enrich me with their long life, and me grace to be in heart no less thankful to receive it than I now am glad in writing to show it; and although I have plenty of matter, here I will stay, for I know you are not quiet to read.

From Cheston (Cheshunt), this present Saturday.

Your Highness' humble daughter,

Elizabeth.

Princess Elizabeth to Katherine Parr[60]

July 31, 1548

Katherine's labor approaches. She will die a little over a month after the penning of this letter.

Although your Highness's letters be most joyful to me in absence, yet considering what pain it is for you to write, your Grace being so sickly, your commendations were enough in my Lord's letter. I much rejoice at your health, with the well-liking of the country, with my humble thanks that your Grace wished me with you till you were weary of that country. Your Highness were like to be cumbered, if I should not depart till I were weary of being with you; although it were the worst soil in the world, your presence would make it pleasant. I cannot reprove my Lord for not doing your commendations in his letter, for he did it; and

---

60. Source: Strickland, *Lives of the Queens of England*, 79.

although he had not, yet I will not complain on him; for he shall be diligent to give me knowledge from time to time how his busy child doth; and if I were at his birth, no doubt I would see him beaten, for the trouble he hath put to you. Master Denny and my lady, with humble thanks, prayeth most entirely for your Grace, praying the Almighty God to send you a most lucky deliverance, and my mistress[61] wisheth no less, giving your Highness most humble thanks for her commendations.

Written with very little leisure this last day of July.

Your humble daughter,

Elizabeth.

Princess Mary to Queen Dowager Katherine Parr[62]

August 9, 1548

Katherine is pregnant. Mary entrusts Lord Marquess of Northampton, Katherine's brother William Parr, with the delivery of her letter.

Madam,

Although I have troubled your Highness with sundry letters, yet that notwithstanding, seeing my Lord Marquis, who hath taken pains to come unto me at this present, intendeth to see your Grace shortly, I could not be satisfied without writing to the same: and especially, because I purpose to-morrow, with the help of God, to begin my journey

61. Katherine Ashley, her governess.
62. Source: Strype, *Ecclesiastical Memorials*, 2.1:60–61; also in Strickland, *Lives of the Queens of England*, 81.

towards Norfolk, where I shall be farther from your Grace. Which journey I have intended since Whitsuntide, but lack of health hath stayed me all this while. Which, although it be as yet unstable, nevertheless I am enforced to remove for a time, hoping, with God's grace, to return again about Mighelmas. At which time, or shortly after, I trust to hear good success of your Grace's great belly. And in the mean while shall desire much to hear of your health, which I pray Almighty God to continue and increase to his pleasure, as much as your own heart can desire. And thus, with my most humble commendations to your Highness, I take my leave of the same, desiring your Grace to take the pains to make my commendation to my Lord Admiral. From Beaulieu, this 9th of August.

Your Highness humble and assured loving daughter,

Mary.

The Lord Protector, Edward Somerset to Thomas Seymour[63]

September 1, 1548

From Thomas Seymour's brother, the Lord Protector of Edward VI, on the occasion of the birth of his daughter.

To our very good lord and brother, the Lord Admiral of England,

After our right hearty recommendations, we are right glad to understand by your letters that the Queen, your bedfellow, hath had a happy hour; and, escaping all danger,

63. Source: Tytler, *England under the Reigns of Edward VI and Mary*, 123–24.

hath made you the father of so pretty a daughter. And although (if it had so pleased God) it would have been both to us, and we suppose also to you, a more joy and comfort if it had been this the first a son; yet the escape of the danger, and the prophecy and good hansell of this to a great sort of happy sons, the which, as you write, we trust no less than to be true, is no small joy and comfort to us, as we are sure it is to you and to her Grace also; to whom you shall make again our hearty commendations, with no less gratulation of [such] good success. Thus we bid you right heartily farewell.

From Sion, the first of Sept. 1548.

Your loving brother,

E. Somerset.

BIBLIOGRAPHY

Augustine of Hippo. *The Works of St. Augustine: A Translation for the 21st Century*. Vol. 1.1, *The Confessions*. Edited by John E. Rotelle. Translated by Maria Boulding. Hyde Park, NY: New City Press, 1997.

Bruce, John, ed. *Correspondence of Matthew Parker, DD: Archbishop of Canterbury, Comprising Letters Written by Him and to him from A.D. 1535, to His Death, A.D. 1575*. Cambridge: The University Press, 1853.

Foxe, John. *The Acts and Monuments of John Foxe: With a Life of the Martyrologist, and Vindication of the Work by the Reverend George Townsend*. Vol. 5. New York: AMS Press, 1965.

Gairdner, James, and R. H. Brodie. *Letters and Papers, Foreign and Domestic, of the Reign of Henry VIII, Preserved in the Public Record Office, the British Museum, and Elsewhere in England*. Vol. 19.1. London: Her Majesty's Stationery Office, 1903.

Green, Mary Anne Everett Wood. *Letters of Royal and Illustrious Ladies of Great Britain, from the Commencement of the Twelfth Century to the Close of the Reign of Queen Mary*. Vol. 3. London: Henry Colburn, 1846.

Halliwell, James Orchard. *Letters of the Kings of England, Now First Collected from the Originals in Royal Archives, and from Other Authentic Sources, Private as Well as Public*. London: Henry Colburn, 1846.

Haugaard, William P. "Katherine Parr: The Religious Convictions of a Renaissance Queen." *Renaissance Quarterly* 22 (1969): 346–59.

Haynes, Samuel, AM. *A Collection of State Papers Relating to Affairs in the Reigns of King Henry VIII, King Edward VI, Queen Mary, and Queen Elizabeth, from the Year 1542–1570, Transcribed from Original Letters and Other Authentik Memorials, Never Before Published, Left by William Cecill Lord Burghle*. Vol. 1. London: William Bowyer, 1740.

Hoffman, C. Fenno, Jr. "Catherine Parr as a Woman of Letters." *Huntington Library Quarterly* 23 (1960): 349–67.

Hume, Martin. *The Wives of Henry the Eighth and the Parts They Played in History*. London: Eveleigh Nash, 1905.

Innes, A. D. *A History of the British Nation, from the Earliest Times to the Present Day*. London: T. C. & E. C. Jack, 1912.

James, Susan E. *Kateryn Parr: The Making of a Queen*. Aldershot, England: Ashgate, 1999.

Latimer, Hugh. *The Works of Hugh Latimer, Sometime Bishop of Worcester, Martyr, 1555*. Edited by George Elwes Corrie. Cambridge: Parker Society and University Press, 1844.

Lodge, Edmund. *Portraits of Illustrious Personages of Great Britain, Engraved from Authentic Pictures in the Galleries of the Nobility and the Public Collections of the Country with Biographical and Historical Memoirs of Their Lives and Actions*. Vol. 7. London: Harding and Lepard, 1835.

MacCulloch, Diarmaid. *Thomas Cranmer: A Life*. New Haven: Yale, 1996.

Maitland, S. R. *The Reformation in England*. New York: John Lane Company, 1906.

Marcus, Leah S., Janel Mueller, and Mary Beth Rose. *Elizabeth I: Collected Works*. Chicago: University of Chicago Press, 2000.

Markham, Sir Clement R. *King Edward VI: His Life and Character*. London: Smith, Elder & Co., 1907.

Martienssen, Anthony. *Queen Katherine Parr*. New York: McGraw-Hill, 1973.

Matthew, H. C. G., and Brian Harrison, eds. *Oxford Dictionary of National Biography: From the Earliest Times to the Year 2000*. Vol. 42, *Osborne-Pate*. New York: Oxford University Press, 2004.

McConica, J. K. *English Humanists and Reformation Politics under Henry VIII and Edward VI*. Oxford: Clarendon Press, 1965.

Mueller, Janel. "Devotion as Difference: Intertextuality in Queen Katherine Parr's Prayers or Meditations (1545)." *Huntington Library Quarterly* 53 (1990): 171–97.

———. *The Early Modern Englishwoman: A Facsimile Library of Essential Works, Part 1: Printed Writings, 1500–1640*. Vol. 3, *Katherine Parr*. Aldershot, England: Scolar Press, 1996.

Nichols, John Gough. *Literary Remains of King Edward the Sixth, Edited from His Autograph Manuscripts with Historical Notes and a Biographical Memoir*. Vol. 1. New York: Burt Franklin, 1857.

———. *Literary Remains of King Edward the Sixth, Edited from His Autograph Manuscripts with Historical Notes and a Biographical Memoir*. Vol. 2. New York: Burt Franklin, 1857.

Parr, Katherine. *Prayers or Meditations Wherein the Mind Is Stirred Patiently to Suffer All Afflictions Here, to Set at Nought the Vain Prosperity of This World, and Always to Long for the Everlasting Felicity. Collected Out of Certain Holy Works, by the Most Virtuous and Gracious Princess Catherine, Queen of England, France, and Ireland*. London: Thomas Berthelet, 1547.

———. *The Lamentation or Complaint of a Sinner*. London: Edwarde Whitchurche, 1548.

Religious Tract Society. *Writings of Edward the Sixth, William Hugh, Queen Catherine Parr, Anne Askew, Lady Jane Grey, Hamilton, and Balnaves.* London: The Religious Tract Society, 1836.

Starkey, David. *Six Wives: The Queens of Henry VIII.* New York: Harper-Collins, 2003.

Strickland, Agnes. *Lives of the Queens of England from the Norman Conquest with Anecdotes of Their Courts.* Vol. 4. Philadelphia: Lea and Blanchard, 1848.

Strype, John. *Ecclesiastical Memorials Relating Chiefly to Religion and the Reformation of It and the Emergencies of the Church of England under King Henry VIII, King Edward VI, and Queen Mary I with Large Appendixes, Containing Original Papers, Records, &c.* Vol. 2.1. Oxford: Clarendon Press, 1822.

———. *Ecclesiastical Memorials Relating Chiefly to Religion and the Reformation of It and the Emergencies of the Church of England under King Henry VIII, King Edward VI, and Queen Mary I with Large Appendixes, Containing Original Papers, Records, &c.* Vol. 2.2. Oxford: Clarendon Press, 1822.

Tytler, Patrick Fraser. *England under the Reigns of Edward VI and Mary with the Contemporary History of Europe Illustrated in a Series of Original Letters Never Before Printed.* Vol. 1. London: Richard Bentley, 1839.

Warnicke, Retha M. *Women of the English Renaissance and Reformation.* Westport, CT: Greenwood Press, 1983.

Weir, Alison. *The Six Wives of Henry VIII.* New York: Grove Press, 1991.

Zahl, Paul F. M. *Five Women of the English Reformation.* Grand Rapids: Eerdmans, 2001.

About the Illustrations

1.1 Katherine Parr Timeline.

1.2 Queen Katherine Parr, engraving by John Cochran after the painting by Hans Holbein. From *King Edward VI: His Life and Character*, by Sir Clement R. Markham. London: Smith, Elder & Co., 1907.

1.3 The Hierarchy of the Sciences as Conceived by Medieval Thought, from the Berri Bible. From the bottom left, second row up, Avicenna, Socrates, and Plato. At the top of the hierarchy are God the Father and the crucified Christ. From *A History of the British Nation, from the Earliest Times to the Present Day*, by A. D. Innes. London: T. C. & E. C. Jack, 1912.

1.4 Thomas Cranmer (1489–1556), Archbishop of Canterbury, engraving by W. Holl after the painting by "Gerbicus Flicciis," or Gerlach Flicke (ca. 1545). From *King Edward VI: His Life and Character*, by Sir Clement R. Markham. London: Smith, Elder & Co., 1907. "From an Engraving by W. Holl after the Painting by 'Gerbicus Flicciis' in the British Museum."

1.5 Henry VIII, from a portrait by Hans Holbein (ca. 1542). From *The Wives of Henry the Eighth and the Parts*

They Played in History, by Martin Hume. London: Eveleigh Nash, 1905.

1.6 Stephen Gardiner (ca. 1483–1555), Bishop of Winchester, engraving by P. A. Ganst. From *The Reformation in England*, by S. R. Maitland. New York: John Lane Company, 1906.

1.7 Chancellor Thomas Wriothesley (1505–50), first Earl of Southampton, engraved by H. Robinson. From *Portraits of Illustrious Personages of Great Britain, Engraved from Authentic Pictures in the Galleries of the Nobility and the Public Collections of the Country with Biographical and Historical Memoirs of Their Lives and Actions*, vol. 7, by Edmund Lodge. London: Harding and Lepard, 1835. "Engraved by H. Robinson. Thomas Wriothesley, Earl of Southampton. OB. 1667. From the original of Sir Peter Lely in the collection of his Grace, the Duke of Bedford."

1.8 King Edward VI (1537–53), engraving by H. T. Ryall after the painting by Petworth (ca. 1547). From *King Edward VI: His Life and Character*, by Sir Clement R. Markham. London: Smith, Elder & Co., 1907.

1.9 Thomas, Lord Seymour of Sudeley (ca. 1508–49), engraving by Thomas Wright after the painting by Hans Holbein. From *King Edward VI: His Life and Character*, by Sir Clement R. Markham. London: Smith, Elder & Co., 1907.

2.1 Title page of *Prayers or Meditations*. From *Prayers or Meditations Wherein the Mind Is Stirred Patiently to Suffer All Afflictions Here, to Set at Nought the Vain Prosperity of This World, and Always to Long for the Everlasting Felicity. Collected*

Out of Certain Holy Works, by the Most Virtuous and Gracious Princess Catherine, Queen of England, France, and Ireland. London: Thomas Berthelet, 1547.

3.1 Title page of *The Lamentation or Complaint of a Sinner.* From *The Lamentation or Complaint of a Sinner*, by Katherine Parr, Queen, consort of Henry VIII, King of England. London: Edwarde Whitchurche, 1548.

4.1 A sample of Katherine Parr's handwriting. This is the 1547 letter to Thomas Seymour in which they renew their courtship. From *Annals of Winchcombe and Sudeley*, by Emma Dent. London: John Murray, 1877. "Facsimilie of Katherine Parr's letter to Seymour of Sudeley, accepting his offer of marriage. (Formerly in the collection of Strawberry Hill)."

INDEX OF PERSONS

Brandon G. Withrow (M.A., Trinity Evangelical Divinity School, Ph.D., Westminster Theological Seminary) is Instructor in Historical and Theological Studies at Winebrenner Theological Seminary. He taught at Beeson Divinity School, Samford University. He is the editor of *A Treatise on Regeneration* by Peter van Mastricht and co-author of the five-volume *History Lives* series.

Also in the GUIDED TOUR series

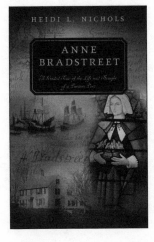

by Heidi L. Nichols
Price: $13.99
To order, visit
www.prpbooks.com
or call
1(800) 631-0094

"This book does a masterful job of performing the task identified in the subtitle—it is a guided tour of the life and work of Anne Bradstreet, conducted by a wonderfully talented tour guide. For anyone wishing to acquire or renew an acquaintance with Anne Bradstreet, this is the book of choice."

— LELAND RYKEN

"Puritan pioneer Anne Bradstreet, solid believer, ardent wife, faithful mother, wise woman, and gifted poetess, is a lady well worth meeting. Dr. Nichols arranges that meeting beautifully in these pages, and merits our gratitude for doing so."

— J. I. PACKER

"Nichols not only illuminates the poet's life and social context, she makes it possible for a new generation to savor Anne Bradstreet's own words and to share the sorrows, joy, and hope of her inner journey."

— CHARLES HAMBRICK-STOWE

Also in the GUIDED TOUR series

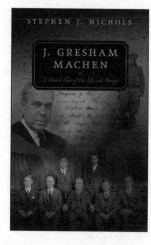

by Stephen J. Nichols
Price: $13.99
To order, visit
www.prpbooks.com
or call
1(800) 631-0094

"Nichols has done a fine job of presenting an accessible introduction to the life and thought of J. Gresham Machen. Nichols offers lucid expositions and fresh interpretations based on his own research."

—GEORGE M. MARSDEN

"J. Gresham Machen's writing was as clear as his arguments were persuasive. Nichols has accomplished the rare feat of making Machen even more accessible. For readers unfamiliar with Machen, this is the perfect appetizer to the feast of further study in Machen's writings. For those more knowledgeable, this will be a reliable reference."

—D. G. HART

"Nichols has provided an accessible gateway to conservative Presbyterianism's most stalwart defender in the tumultuous 1920s. His admiring portrait reminds us of Machen's probing scholarship, his trenchant analysis of modernism, and his attempts to further the Christian world and life view in American culture.

—ANDREW HOFFECKER

Also in the GUIDED TOUR *series*

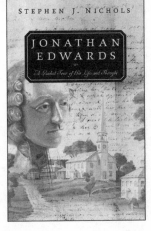

by Stephen J. Nichols
Price: $13.99
To order, visit
www.prpbooks.com
or call
1(800) 631-0094

"A lively and vivid introduction to America's greatest theologian—
the best one yet for use in most churches and Christian colleges."

—DOUGLAS A. SWEENEY

"Nichols is an enthusiastic, experienced, and reliable tour guide to
the theology of Jonathan Edwards. If your experience is like mine,
these pages will make you want to visit Edwards on your own for
frequent and extended periods. An excellent introduction."

—SINCLAIR FERGUSON

"Edwards is still America's greatest theologian, and his works
remain of lasting value to the church. This book is a useful introduction to the great man's message and ministry. Nichols has
chosen his material carefully to help readers begin to understand
Edwards's most important writings."

—PHILIP GRAHAM RYKEN

Also in the GUIDED TOUR series

by Stephen J. Nichols
Price: $13.99
To order, visit
www.prpbooks.com
or call
1(800) 631-0094

"For over half a century Roland Bainton's *Here I Stand* has been the best popular introduction to Luther. Stephen Nichols's engaging volume is in many ways better than Bainton's for this purpose. It deserves to be widely read, and as an unashamed Luther-lover I hope it will be."

—J. I. PACKER

"How do you do a book on everything from training children to hymns to preaching to political conflict—and have it running over with the glorious gospel? Nichols has done it. Be alert: people forget how life-changing the gospel really is—and then are astonished to remember it again as they read Luther."

—D. CLAIR DAVIS

"Since Luther published a printed work about every two weeks of his adult life, there is a lot of ground to cover. But Nichols knows the terrain well and opens up its treasures with a deft touch."

—MARK NOLL